CONT[ENTS]

Planning comes first

Half the work of building a greenhouse is done at the planning stage. Plan it well — and above all, don't make it too small, or you may regret it later. You can always fit a vertical partition inside a longer greenhouse to set up a 'warmer' section later on.

Around 90 per cent of greenhouse buyers choose a width of 8 ft 6 in-10 ft (2.6-3 m) and a length of 10-13 ft (3-4 m). A general-purpose greenhouse is good value: it'll usually have a ridge height of around 7-8 ft (2.1-2.4 m), with the eaves around 5 ft 3 i- 6 ft (1.6-1.8 m) above ground level. Wider greenhouses will be correspondingly taller. Anyone who buys a very small, cheap greenhouse shouldn't really expect too much from it: gardening with your elbows pressed against your ribs is no fun at all. If you want a mini-greenhouse without access, there are various types on the market. They can even be turned to catch the sun. However, they're expensive to buy.

The more ventilators there are, the more choices you will have about how you use your greenhouse in the future. Where it's possible to build a lean-to greenhouse against the wall of a house, you can finish up with something very similar to a conservatory. Besides, it's easy to build a greenhouse extension onto a home that already has a heating system.

High thresholds or steps make it harder to work in and around the greenhouse, especially for older gardeners. If there's a height difference, ramps are a better solution. You can also push a wheelbarrow right up onto the path between the benching (as long as your doorway is wide enough). Besides, good planning means thinking about everything, including the needs of wheelchair users and other disabled people. For them, steps and narrow doors are an insuperable barrier.

A greenhouse is just the thing for this delightful garden, but this type of sliding door does not allow wheelchair access.

Siting the greenhouse

Once your site is fixed you won't be able to change your mind — at least, not if your design calls for solid foundations. When picking your site be sure to think about available light, especially in overcast weather, and at times of the year when the sun is low in the sky. If you're growing shade-loving plants, you can easily use artificial shade to create the diffuse lighting conditions they will need. It's true that lamps can entirely replace natural light, but they're expensive to buy and operate. It's better to use lighting as a supplement where natural light levels are poor. An alternative is the growing room (e.g. a basement or a large cupboard) where all the light is artificial.

'Wind funnels' and 'frost pockets' in the garden will make poor sites for a greenhouse — and if you want to avoid damp foundations, make sure you don't have a drainage problem.

Pick a site where you can link your greenhouse to a mains water supply. If you're going to use this in winter, the pipes must run at a 'frost-free' depth of 2 ft 6 in–3 ft (80–100 cm). The alternative is a temporary connection that can be drained off in winter. A fully functioning greenhouse also needs an electricity supply with at least two waterproof rubber sockets for lighting, humidifier, ventilator, and possibly heating and other appliances. You can connect a greenhouse to your domestic hot water or hot air heating system, but it must have its own circuit. Both feed and return pipes will need to be insulated and professionally laid at a frost-free depth for the run to the greenhouse.

When planning your greenhouse, think carefully about the best site.

Regulations

Before buying a greenhouse, check with your local city, district or county planning office. Ask if you'll need planning permission, and if any aspect of your plans is likely to be affected by local building regulations. These can vary considerably. The right to lay down planning regulations lies with local authorities, so there can even be variations within the same county. However, conservatories or greenhouses attached to a dwelling house will invariably need planning permission, especially if they cover doors or windows.

A number of issues may interest the planning authorities. Where will your greenhouse stand in relation to the boundaries of your property? Will it be visible from neighbouring properties? How are you building it? Will you be using glass or some other material? Will it have its own heater, or will you connect it to your domestic central heating system? Will it be free-standing, or will it form an extension to an existing building? All these points must be clarified beforehand. The same goes for allotments. Some forbid the building of greenhouses, others allow them. The local rules will be in each association's regulations.

Styles

There's a choice of three basic greenhouse styles. Your decision isn't just a matter of personal taste — it will also be governed by local conditions and the way your greenhouse is going to be used in the future.

Span-roof greenhouse

This type of greenhouse has a sloping roof either side of a central ridge. The advantage is that daylight can penetrate from all sides, especially when the greenhouse is free-standing in the garden. In autumn and winter, when the sun is lower in the sky and its light is less intense, this type of greenhouse gives the highest possible light levels inside, especially when the ridge runs east–west. The same applies on overcast days. The side walls also have an effect on internal light levels: the greater the height to the eaves, the better. As well as creating a taller greenhouse, this allows more light to enter from all sides. Artificial shading can produce a more diffuse illumination for plants that have less need of light.

If your greenhouse will be free-standing in the garden, and will mostly be used between spring and autumn, you're normally advised to line it up on a north–south axis. However, orientation is no longer seen as critical, and site conditions and existing buildings often limit your choice. Besides, it's easier to get the most out of low winter light levels when the greenhouse lies on an east–west axis. If site conditions make it possible, you can build a span-roof greenhouse so that one gable end lines up against the wall of your house. This may give you direct access, and make it easier to connect the greenhouse to your central heating system. Large-panel Dutch-type greenhouses with dry-glazing systems are also still available.

In a free-standing greenhouse, you'll need to set the benefits of all-round light penetration against the higher heating costs it will incur. Making the greenhouse an extension of your home means there's one less wall where heat can be lost. And you won't lose a drastic amount of light. Even a free-standing span-roof greenhouse will rarely be flooded with light all the time — neighbouring objects or buildings will often cast shadows over it.

Lean-to greenhouse

This type is built with its long side against a wall, a garage or (preferably) a house.

This arrangement takes up more wall space than a span-

A span-roof greenhouse and two garden frames

Pavilion greenhouses

Pavilion greenhouses have taken an increasing share of the market in recent years. Most have between six and nine sides. They're suitable for raising young plants and ornamentals, including exotic species, but less suitable for growing vegetables. Since this type of greenhouse is usually free-standing, light levels inside it are excellent.

Above *A lean-to greenhouse*
Right *This pavilion-style greenhouse creates an attractive focal point for the garden.*

roof greenhouse with its gable end against the wall. In contrast to the span-roof greenhouse, the lean-to has a single-sided roof. Ideally it should be orientated east–west, with the roof sloping to the south. This allows the best possible light transmission. You can use various pieces of apparatus to moderate unwanted light and heat. Without shading and adequate ventilation, lean-to greenhouses in a south-facing position can easily overheat in summer.

Admittedly the lean-to is only half a greenhouse with a single-sided roof, but it can give full value in use. Here too, it's advisable to keep the eaves as high as possible so you can use the space under the benching at the front of the greenhouse, ideally on the south side.

Construction

The word 'greenhouse' can be used to describe many different buildings. There are differences in style (span-roof, lean-to or pavilion) and in construction (heavy-duty or lightweight). Before deciding on the construction method, you need to think about the way you're going to use the greenhouse. The trend is towards a general-purpose greenhouse.

Heavy-duty structures meet all the demands that can be put on a greenhouse. If they are properly built, they will meet the most stringent requirements of gardeners. The structural sections are normally thicker than those of a lightweight construction, and should last for many years.

The ideal greenhouse is firmly assembled, with individual sections screwed or welded together, and stands on solid foundations. Whether it's been built from scratch or bought in ready-made sections, a greenhouse like this will be well worth the effort.

With a heavy-duty structure you can install virtually any fittings and equipment you are likely to want, including hot-water pipes for heating. It should be easy to connect the greenhouse to your domestic central heating system, provided it's a lean-to, a span-roof type with one gable abutting the house, or a free-standing greenhouse close by — and provided that night-time operation isn't a problem. Ideally the greenhouse should have its own independently controlled heating circuit. It's best to get advice from a good heating engineer.

Choose your equipment for heating, and for regulating the internal climate, with care. A well-designed greenhouse will make your hobby available throughout the year. Your plants will grow, flower and flourish, even in winter. You can take devoted care of particular rarities. With less intense cultivation, you can cut the cost of your vegetables.

Lightweight structures, by definition, usually have less substantial components. They can even be put together from readily available items such as cold frame lights, or rectangular frames covered in polythene. Such structures have all the advantages (and disadvantages) of any do-it-yourself solution.

Like cloches, lightweight structures of this type are easy to move around. They're also quick to assemble (even if you're not a great do-it-yourselfer). If you already have a few

A galvanised steel greenhouse 10 ft (3 m) wide with roof, side and gable vents.

A polythene tunnel 13 ft (4 m) long and 10 ft (3 m) wide with a sliding door.

cold frame lights lying about doing nothing, you may be able to put them together to make a reasonable greenhouse. But do remember that their thick frames will cut out a significant amount of light.

Lightweight structures are inexpensive. For instance, you don't necessarily need a solid, continuous foundation — breeze blocks, beams or foundations laid just at the key points should be enough. But the resulting structures are usually less suitable for year-round gardening. Depending on how they are built, and how they are covered (e.g. with glass, plastic or polythene sheeting, or with adapted cold frame lights), they aren't usually all that stable. And if you *do* want to use them throughout the year, they'll need more in the way of heating.

Even so, lightweight structures *can* easily be heated, at least enough to keep them frost-free in early spring and late autumn. Make full use of them at these times. Start by raising seedlings, go on to fill the space with cucumbers, tomatoes and peppers, and then make autumn sowings of lettuce, kohl rabi, corn salad and other plants. That should give you plenty of scope for success.

A well-built light-weight greenhouse covered with plastic sheeting — also called a polythene tunnel — can often provide an introduction to greenhouse gardening. Newer types of 'thermal' polythene reduce heat loss and avoid excessive condensation; they can provide an ideal environment for plant growth. Double skinning of polythene structures provides a warm environment at low cost, entirely suitable for overwintering balcony and container-grown plants.

Mixed vegetables in a polythene tunnel.

The parts of a greenhouse

A greenhouse is made up of various structural elements:

The **roof glazing bars** connect the ridge and the eaves and support the glazing.

It is important to have **vents** in the roof, and ideally at the sides as well. Ventilation reduces the temperature in the greenhouse, creates good air circulation and

The **ridge** is where the sloping slides of the roof meet.

The long sides are connected by the **gable ends**. Span-roof greenhouses have only one gable end if they are put up with one short side against another building. Lean-to greenhouses have one long side and two gable ends.

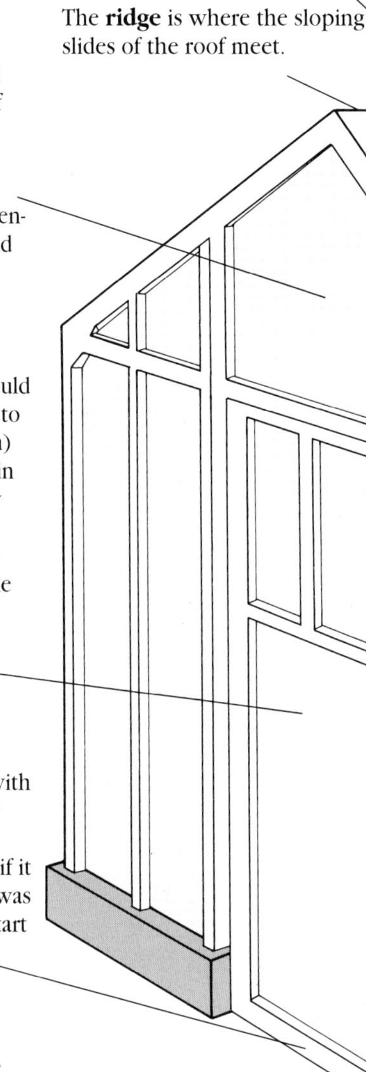

The **door** is set in one gable end. To avoid heat loss it should always be a tight fit. It needs to be 6 ft 3 in–6 ft 6 in (1.9–2 m) in height and 2 ft 4 in–3 ft 3 in (0.7–1 m) wide. You can buy either side-hinged or sliding doors: sliding doors have the advantage that they don't take up much room.

Ideally, the **entry** should be level with the central path inside the greenhouse, and with the ground outside. A higher entry is useful if it stops rainwater from getting in — but if it does get in, the greenhouse was built in the wrong place to start with.

Not all greenhouses have the structure illustrated here — there are many other variations.

controls humidity. Make sure you can secure the vents in different positions to vary the size of the openings and regulate the flow of air.

It's best to have **side vents** (to let in cool air) *and* **roof vents** (to let warm air escape). In summer ventilation is vital to avoid overheating and admit fresh air. It must still work even when there's no wind. With effective ventilation, the air inside a greenhouse is renewed about twenty times in an hour.

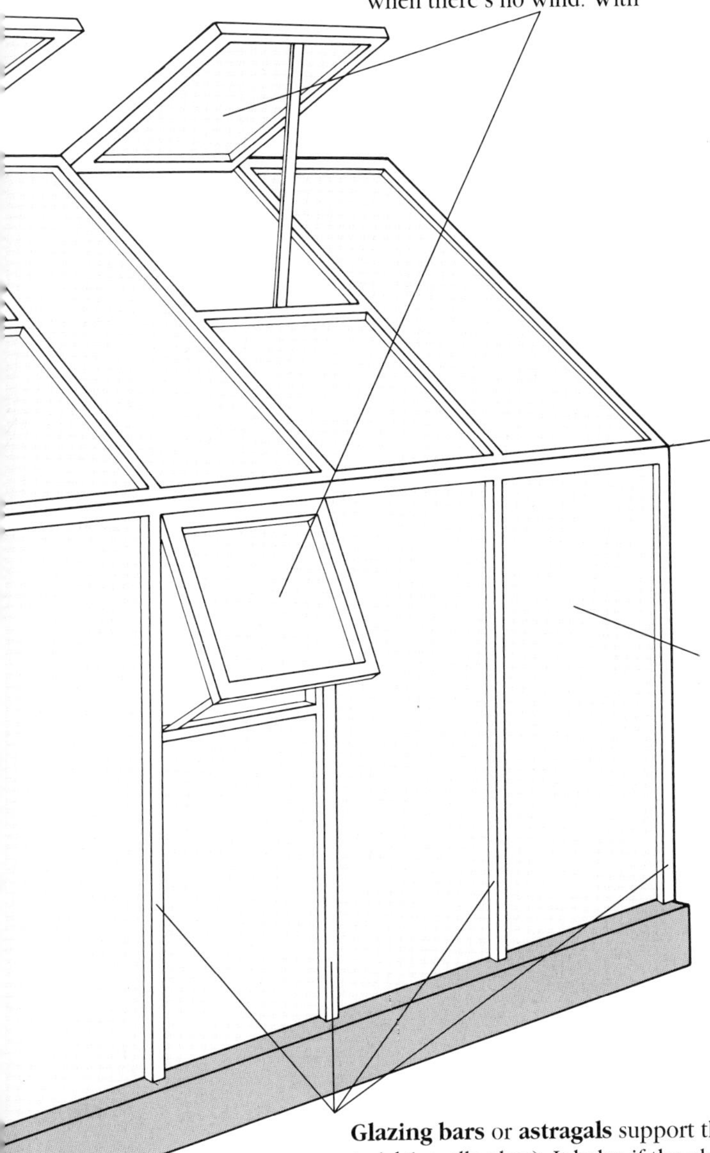

The more **ventilators** in a greenhouse, the better. Ideally these should be louvre vents in the side walls and gable ends: they're more effective, less liable to wind damage and less likely to cause an obstruction.

Longitudinal or horizontal **girders** aren't usually needed in smaller greenhouses. The same is true of cross-braces.

The **eaves** are at the junction of the side wall and the roof. The roof and wall glazing bars are attached to them, as are the gutters and downpipes (if they are fitted).

The **long side wall** is the part between eaves and base. Span greenhouses have two such walls, lean-tos only one. Vertical side walls are preferable: sloping walls reduce the width in the upper part of the greenhouse as well as restricting the surface area of the benching. However, if the greenhouse ridge runs east–west, sloping sides have light transmission advantages, especially in winter.

Glazing bars or **astragals** support the roof and hold the glazing material (usually glass). It helps if the glazing system is the sealed type.

Foundations

A well-constructed greenhouse depends on a good foundation that will hold firm in stormy weather, and be completely unaffected by a cold spell.

The depth and nature of the foundations vary according to the type of greenhouse. On average, the trench is dug to a depth of 12 in (30 cm) and about the same width. You may need a deeper trench where the ground isn't fully consolidated. Run the cement into the trench and dump it reasonably level with a dumping board. For smaller greenhouses a shallower and narrower trench may be sufficient. Some greenhouses depend on anchor cleats cemented firmly into the ground at an appropriate depth. Ideally this should be in addition to a firm cement base to take the weight of the greenhouse.

Greenhouse manufacturers will invariably provide a base plan. The upper edge of the foundations should slope towards the outside, so that any rainwater will flow away from the base. With brick or block bases it's important to stop rising damp; this is achieved by laying a damp-proof membrane where the base of the wall joins the foundation. However, many modern greenhouses are glass-to-ground, with kick-boards at the base and anchor cleats.

An essential stage: checking the foundations with a spirit level.

Do-it-yourself kits

Greenhouses are available ready to assemble in all the usual materials, and in a full range of models from simple to sophisticated. Kits can also allow you to extend your greenhouse. Most manufacturers supply interior fittings. Some may also be able to provide interior equipment that does much of the regular work automatically.

As fuel costs continue to rise, manufacturers are making ever greater efforts to provide well-insulated structures. Sealed or bar-cap glazing systems with plastic edging instead of overlaps on the side will help to ensure minimum heat loss and eliminate drips and draughts.

Nowadays there's a huge range of greenhouses available. With so many to choose from, you must be prepared to make critical comparisons. Manufacturers who offer price cuts and special offers don't always live up to their promises. Putting things right afterwards — even if it's possible — could cost you more than you thought you'd saved, as well as causing aggravation. If you're seriously interested in buying a greenhouse, don't just look at the glossy brochures. Look at a good selection of real greenhouses in detail. When

Four stages in assembly: putting together the gable; aligning the components; sliding in the panes; a final check.

comparing, it's just as important to think about eaves and ridge heights as to choose between straight or sloping walls and ranges of available equipment.

The most important factor is the general stability and the quality of the glazing system: even in a strong gale the glass should not be loosened and the structure should not vibrate. If you're looking at a greenhouse, push against the side: it can be very revealing. Structures more than about 8 ft (2.5 m) wide should have cross braces above head height to avoid damage by snow load or excess movement in a high wind. You should also note that the manufacturer may not supply enough vents to air the greenhouse properly, especially if it's a lean-to set against a south-facing wall.

Building your own greenhouse

Not for the novice

DIY isn't everybody's cup of tea, and can be far from simple for the inexperienced. A scratch-built structure that turns out to be faulty can become a source of constant aggravation. There's definitely something to be said for a ready-made greenhouse. It comes with detailed instructions and only needs to be put together — the building-kit system makes construction easy. Just screw the components together and put them up. It's straightforward, and it's easy to produce a successful result.

Materials of different weights

Anyone who's clever with their hands will probably enjoy building their own greenhouse. A polythene-covered greenhouse could be ideal for your first attempt. You can create an adequate structure with a lightweight framework of wood or steel; use angle-iron or T-section for a glass-clad structure, or tubular steel bent into a hoop shape for polythene. Bear in mind that 1 sq ft of glass weighs 24 oz if it is 3 mm thick (and 1 m^2 of 3 mm glass weighs 7 kg). By contrast, sheets of thick plastic such as polycarbonate, acrylic or PVC weigh only a fraction of this, and standard grades of polythene (720 gauge) weigh even less.

Polythene structures

Polythene structures are fairly easy to build on wooden frameworks; tack the polythene to the frame with wooden laths or battens to avoid local stress points. However, you can build a much more stable structure with galvanised steel hoops (the diameter varies according to the width and length of the structure). The polythene will tend to degrade because of UV radiation and chafing against the hoops, but you can largely prevent this by using **hot-spot tape** — a white sticky-backed material which you apply to the outside of the hoops. You can either dig the polythene into the ground, or support it with aluminium gripstrip at ground level. You can even fit side ventilation by using double gripstrip with a netting base. Stretch the polythene tightly over the hoops to prevent flapping.

Basic frameworks

You can make rudimentary greenhouses from a variety of materials including steel, aluminium and (of course) wood. Existing cold frame lights can be fitted together on a supporting framework of angle iron or wood to form a functional structure. This is often done to protect crops or flowers from excessive rain — particularly if you have aspirations in the local flower show, and want to ensure that your prize exhibits are unmarked. Because of the basic nature of this kind of structure, there's no need to go to great lengths to seal up the joins.

Plastic sheeting must be protected from mechanical damage, e.g. being rubbed against the framework by the wind. Putting foam strips over metal parts where they support the plastic will prevent damage from overheating in bright sunshine. If you don't need the polythene for a while, store it in a dark place: it's the ultraviolet rays in sunlight that do the most damage.

Types of greenhouse

The way you use a greenhouse depends, at least in part, on the type of greenhouse it is. There are four basic types of ground-level greenhouse; the others are all derived from them. There's also the so-called **stove house**, likewise available in several variations. Greenhouses are classified according to the way their side walls are constructed. When you're deciding which type of greenhouse you want, start by thinking about what you intend to do with it.

Unhindered by masonry, light penetrates a greenhouse from all directions. This kind of structure — a general-purpose greenhouse with many possible uses — offers the best value for money.

Ground-level greenhouses

It's not a good idea to start out with fixed ideas about how you will use your greenhouse, and then settle for one that can only be used in a limited way. For instance, if you decided to raise seedlings in a stove house you'd probably soon feel the need for a little more scope. A general-purpose greenhouse with glass or plastic sides from base to eaves is a much less restricting choice. It can be heated all year round, and the structure imposes no limitations in use. With no masonry to get in the way, light can enter from all sides. It really doesn't matter if the plants stand on benching or shelves, or simply grow in the borders.

If the side walls are half glass and half masonry or concrete, the space under the benching can only be used for forcing plants such as rhubarb and chicory.

If the base (or the masonry) reaches no more than a quarter of the way up the greenhouse between the ground and the eaves, daylight can still penetrate under the benching. This means that plants can be grown there such as chives, parsley and rhubarb. On the benching itself, where there is no obstacle to the light, you can grow seedlings and ornamental plants. If there's no benching you can plant kohl rabi, cucumbers and tomatoes in the borders.

If the side walls are half masonry and half glass, the space below the benching will be virtually unusable. It's bound to be dark down there, particularly in the winter, when light levels are low in any case. This means you can use the space to grow a limited range of plants that don't need much light, e.g. rhubarb and chicory. On the benching, by contrast, you can grow whatever you like. This type of greenhouse is most often used to grow seedlings.

Houses with walls built entirely of brick or cement (where the cement is often a continuation of the base) are very unsatisfactory, because light can only get in through the roof. Limited light restricts the choice of plants: it's even hard to grow seedlings when the only light comes from above. Shade-loving plants will thrive and it may also suit container-grown plants during the winter. In other respects no greenhouse could be further from the general-purpose ideal. The dubious advantage of reduced heating costs is no compensation for the lack of light.

Stove houses

With a stove house, only the roof and the sides are above ground. The sides may be made of glass, or they may simply be a continuation of the foundation. They can be fairly high or quite low. A downward flight of steps gives access. It may be a good idea to cover the entrance — if you don't, water can get down the steps after heavy rainfall.

Stove houses can be built in both span-roof and lean-to styles when heat conservation is a critical issue. Their use is limited to raising seedlings, general propagation, and cultivating low-growing plants. At one time this kind of greenhouse was used for cucumbers and melons. If the greenhouse has glass sides you'll be able to cultivate lettuce, kohl rabi and radishes.

Stove houses provide acceptable, safe conditions for overwintering many plants, at low cost, i.e. with sufficient heat to keep out frost. Pelargoniums, fuchsias and dahlia tubers can be kept here; so can gladioli corms and the bulbs of other garden plants. It's difficult to overwinter taller plants unless you remove the benching, but this could be tricky. Most stove houses have concrete or masonry retaining walls either side of the central path.

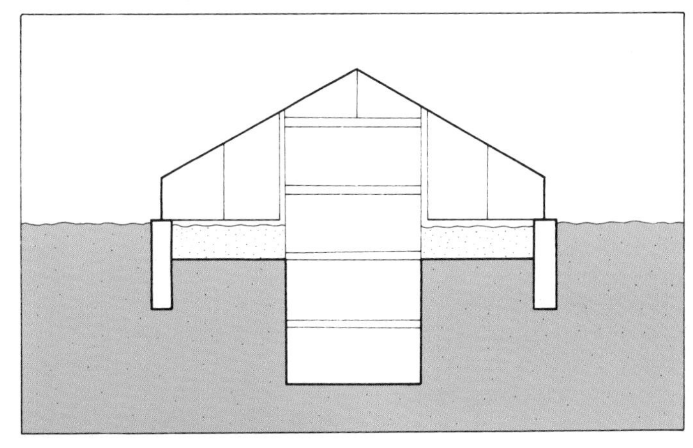

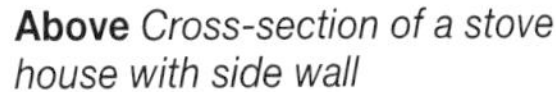

Above *Cross-section of a stove house with side wall*

Left *This stove house blends beautifully into the garden around it. The steps are bounded by a palisade. It's very attractive — but proper drainage is essential.*

It's completely wrong to choose a greenhouse just because it's the cheapest you can find. You need to think about the relationship between price and performance. Greenhouse exhibits at garden festivals give you the chance to compare different models, as do the major gardening exhibitions in Chelsea, Southport and Harrogate. Some manufacturers also provide their own exhibits to show how their designs stand up to actual use. These do, at least, make it possible to compare the ranges offered by different companies.

Building materials compared

Wood

Wood is a very versatile material for building greenhouses, but it's important to use a high-quality wood (e.g. western red cedar) that has natural resistance to decay. If you're using Baltic red wood it must be pressure-treated. Tropical hardwoods are seldom used for greenhouses these days, although they're popular for expensive conservatories. These woods are not for the DIY enthusiast: aside from their cost, they are hard to work with.

The best approach to building a wooden greenhouse is to seek out a suitably-sized wooden structure in a neighbour's garden, or in a display (e.g. at your garden centre or in an exhibition). Measure up the wooden sections and make a note of the design. As long as you have adequate tools you can then shape the wood as necessary, or you may be able to order suitably shaped wood from a sawmill. Wooden

This greenhouse looks good, but the thick wooden components mean that some light is being lost. However, for general growing activities this isn't a problem.

The most effective method of protecting timber is a pressure treatment. The pores of the wood are opened under vacuum, and preservative is forced in under pressure. The amateur can partly impregnate wood with oil preservatives or water-soluble salts, either by painting them on or by immersing the timber in the preservative. If you apply coloured paints the humidity of the wood should not be above 15 per cent, because these paints largely prevent the wood from breathing. Always use products that don't damage plants.

greenhouses can readily be constructed from Dutch lights, which are clamped together. This involves buying the Dutch lights from a supplier and using hinges (or clamps) as required, though the end-gable sections of Dutch-light greenhouses will need some modification.

If you're using wood to build a greenhouse, try to keep the sections as slender as possible, taking into account the need for structural strength: thick, clumsy wooden sections will obviously restrict the entry of sunlight.

An aluminium span-roof greenhouse coated brown.

Steel

Instead of wood, you could work with steel — but there's a problem. If it's galvanised, as it should be, cutting and drilling it leaves the way open for rust (though much can be done to prevent this with modern paints). Steel is a very strong metal and will certainly make a strong greenhouse. However, because it is difficult to shape, glazing systems tend to be very rudimentary, involving the use of putty or plastic glazing strips. If the glass is not properly sealed it can all too easily be loosened in windy weather. Non-hardening bitumens combined with plastic clips provide an ideal way of sealing the glass.

It is absolutely vital to treat the steel effectively, whether by galvanising or by some other means. In fact, steel houses are not, at present, very popular in the United Kingdom, mainly because they are vulnerable to rust and difficult to glaze effectively. This is why aluminium has largely taken over.

Aluminium

Aluminium is an ideal material for building greenhouses because it has a long life and it isn't vulnerable to rust. It can also be extruded in various ways to form effective astragals and other fitments. Electrolytic surface treatment of aluminium can produce white, brown, and other surface colours, but natural aluminium is the most widely used material in the United Kingdom. Many aluminium greenhouses can be bought in kit form. This gives great scope to the DIY enthusiast, especially in cases where the manufacturer provides detailed erection plans.

With aluminium glazing bars you get the benefits of a dry glazing system that doesn't require putty. This has several advantages. If a pane of glass breaks you can repair it quickly and easily. More importantly, you can buy an energy-saving seal for the glazing bars: it takes the form of removable, continuous plastic bar-caps. These largely put a stop to the exchange of heat through the metal, which will otherwise provide a bridge for the cold. The energy saving is around 6 per cent.

Glazing methods and materials

Single layer

GLASS

Aesthetically speaking, wooden greenhouses, especially those built in red cedar, make a most attractive addition to the garden. Despite the introduction of plastic glazing materials such as PVC, acrylic and polycarbonate, glass still remains the most popular form of glazing for greenhouses. The type of glass used is called **horticultural glass**: it's supplied in various thicknesses, but only two are useful to greenhouse builders:

Designation	Thickness in mm	Weight in oz/sq in (kg/m^2)
Medium thickness	3	24 (7)
Double thickness	4	32 (9)

'Frosted' horticultural glass is not transparent but translucent, and best called that. One side is flat, the other knobbly. With plain glass, the rays of light pass straight through; with translucent glass, the light becomes diffused. Translucent glass is fitted with the knobbly side to the inside.

Both types of glass will let through 89-92 per cent of visible light falling on them at right angles. The most usual size of pane is 24 × 24 in (60 × 60 cm). Various other sizes such as 20 × 18 in (50 × 45 cm) and 55 × 28.75 in (142 × 73 cm) for Dutch light greenhouses are available.

Smaller panes need more glazing bars, and this, in turn, leads to loss of light. Depending on the percentage of construction material (i.e. wood or metal) light levels can be reduced by up to 30 per cent, especially if the greenhouse is badly sited as well.

Putty may be used to fix glass onto steel or wooden glazing bars, but is no longer popular. Mastic or plastic strips are often used these days. Do remember that putty won't fix the panes in place; it's simply a way of sealing the junction between the glass and the glazing bar. To fix them you'll need brass sprigs attached to the glazing bars, and storm clips over the glass. Don't fasten the panes rigidly in place; they need a little room to move, or the glass will break.

Dry glazing on an aluminium glazing bar with a PVC bar cap — especially useful in exposed areas.

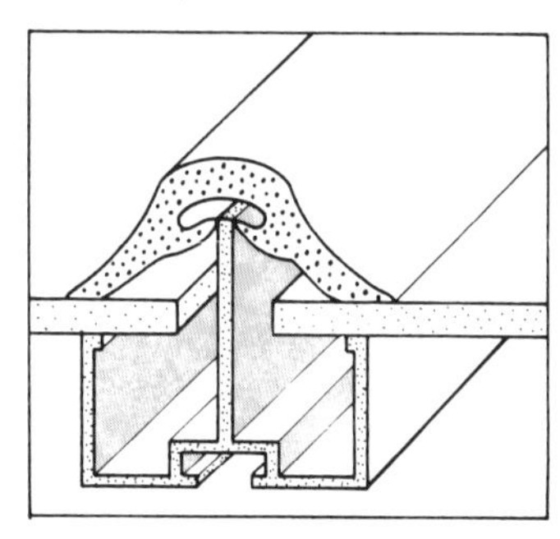

Aluminium glazing bars don't require putty, so glazing (and replacing broken panes) is quick and easy. This 'dry glazing' system may also save more energy, because the glazing bars can be covered with a continuous plastic bar cap that prevents draughts and heat loss. The panes are laid into plastic glazing strips which have been pressed into place on the glazing bars. Low-cost greenhouses have a simple clip system: it's reasonably satisfactory, but not good for an exposed situation.

Even a polythene tunnel offers plenty of scope for different plants.

PLASTIC

Plastic is second in importance only to glass, mainly because of its use in polythene tunnels. Plastic sheeting isn't a substitute for glass, but it is a useful supplement. Many a greenhouse gardener has started with just a polythene tunnel and gone on to build a proper glasshouse.

The main form of plastic sheeting used is polyethylene (polythene), which has some environmental advantages compared with polyvinyl chloride (PVC).

Plastic sheeting will last longer if it's kept in a dark place when you're not using it. 720 gauge polythene will transmit 80–85 per cent of the total light that falls on it, and newer forms with built-in anti-drip features will exceed this, as they are very clear. As well as clear polythene, there are various forms of polythene netting giving different percentages of shade. They can also be used as wind breaks, or to give side or end ventilation in polythene or conventional greenhouses.

Woven sheet and **steel lattice sheeting** (which is plastic bonded either side of a wire mesh) will both last longer, but because they're more expensive they aren't used as often. The lattice will also reduce the amount of light that is transmitted.

Fibreglass reinforced polyester (GRP) is easily identified by the glass fibres embedded in it. It transmits about 85–89 per cent of the direct light that falls on it. It's stable, lightweight, largely hail-proof, and easy to use. The top layer is specially treated with a sealant that prevents (or at least delays) loss of resin from the surface caused by exposure to the sun. It's used a lot in hot countries to reduce solar radiation and to avoid damage by sandblasting.

Sheets of polyvinyl chloride (PVC) around 1 mm thick are used to glaze greenhouses. They are very suitable for DIY projects, and let through about 90 per cent of the light. Moulded sheets are also available, and offer a wide choice of deeper or shallower corrugations. You can also buy trapezium-shaped sections to use at the gables. Seal them with plastic edging strip shaped to match.

A greenhouse can be made using various forms of plastic sheeting such as polycarbonate, acrylic or PVC.

Insulating roofing materials

DOUBLE GLAZING

As heating costs continue to rise, more and more gardeners are starting to think about improving their greenhouse insulation to provide a warmer growing regime at lower cost.

Bear in mind that if snow can't slide off, it's less likely to melt away quickly on a double-glazed roof. If the insulation is efficient (or the interior temperature is low) it may simply lie where it is. This puts a strain on the structure and reduces the light available to your plants. Even if your greenhouse is only single-glazed, it should be kept free of snow.

Double-glazed glass panes come in various forms, but are not widely used in the British Isles because of their cost and weight. However, they are used for up-market conservatories. A form of double glazing is often

Disadvantages of overlapping panes: dirt collects and draughts can penetrate where the panes meet. Continuous panes are preferable.

used for greenhouse walls, where the extra weight of another sheet of glass is not a problem. Some are welded together at the edges, and the space between the layers is filled with air or carbon dioxide. In sealed double glazing the two panes are held a critical distance apart using special adhesives.

With all these systems, it's worth remembering that each pane will weigh twice as much as its single-glazed equivalent. This puts extra weight on the structure, which needs to be firm and stable. A factory-made greenhouse or conservatory designed for double glazing will have the necessary stability built in. But be careful — don't try any DIY 'improvements' to structures that weren't designed for double glazing. You can give them quite adequate insulation by attaching bubble plastic to the inside of the frame.

TWIN-WALL POLYCARBONATE AND TRIPLE-WALL POLYCARBONATE

Twin-wall and triple-wall polycarbonate sheets are made from various different materials under various different trade names.

Double-channelled sheets have a thermal conductivity of about 3 W/m^2/K (3 watts per square metre per degree Kelvin) by themselves; when you include the whole greenhouse structure, this rises to 4 W/m^2/K. The estimated energy saving by using the double-skinned construction is 40 per cent.

By far the most popular form of greenhouse insulation is to line the inside of the greenhouse with bubble polythene. This can be tacked onto the framework of wooden greenhouses with a staple gun and a pad of cardboard to avoid local stress. Special fitting clips are available for aluminium greenhouses. It's not a good idea to cover over the ventilators to the extent that they can't be opened.

Double-skinned polythene structures come in various forms. The cheapest and most effective calls for two polythene covers fitted slackly enough to let them expand and stay apart under the pressure from a small fan. This must run constantly. The Serac greenhouse offers another type of double skinning using panels based on Tedlar, a very clear plastic material. You can even buy a bubble greenhouse which has no framework at all; the structure is kept inflated with a fan. It needs special double doors to prevent deflation when you enter or leave. All plastic-covered structures, including double-skin types, are vulnerable to damage by hail.

Hobby greenhouses, like commercial greenhouses, are vulnerable to storm damage. Despite increasingly rigorous schedules, some insurance companies are still prepared to offer cover for glass panes and plastic glazing materials against hail and storm damage, including damage from the weight of snow or ice.

The inner life of the greenhouse

What would a greenhouse be without its interior fittings? To use it properly and exploit all the possibilities for raising plants, you need much more than a simple glass- or plastic-covered shell.

Exactly *what* you need will depend on the way you intend to use your greenhouse. From spring to autumn it's certainly possible to raise plants without any special equipment, but only to a limited extent.

First comes the staging or benching. Benching is indispensable for propagation and for pot plants. The plants are closer to the light and you don't need to keep bending.

Benching should be about 32–40 in (80–100 cm) high. A lower height of 26–28 in (65–70 cm) is usable if you intend putting seed boxes on top of it. The width of the bench depends on the width of your greenhouse. If the greenhouse is 10 ft (3 m) wide and the central path is 2 ft 6 in (75 cm) wide, then the bench either side will be 3 ft 3 in (1 m) wide. Benching shouldn't be wider than 3 ft (90 cm); this allows easy access to the back. Leave a space between the bench and the outside wall of the greenhouse for air circulation.

Below and right *Interior fittings offer scope for many different uses: wall-mounted and hanging shelves, pots and boxes on the benching, plants underneath, and vegetables and ornamentals in the borders (though plants under benches tend to get drawn due to lack of light).*

Bench tops can be made of various materials including weldmesh, aluminium and wooden slats. If a bench is made of solid wood it should be lined with polythene to prevent rapid deterioration, especially where it is to be used for propagation.

If the bench has raised edges about 4-6 in (10-15 cm) high it can take a layer of soil or compost. This means that plants such as radishes and lettuce can be grown directly on the bench. If a greenhouse with a good eaves height is used mainly for growing vegetables, you don't need benching. There should be enough light coming in to reach the ground.

In this case, planting and sowing are done straight into the borders. In a polythene tunnel this will be the usual procedure, unless you're using it to raise plants. One variation is to install benching on only one side of the greenhouse, leaving a clear border on the other side.

A greenhouse can be partitioned to create two areas that are kept at different temperatures. You can then fit the warm area with benching, and grow plants directly in the borders in the cool area.

Benching can be fitted at any time, not just when the greenhouse is built. You might also consider using movable benching, and putting it alternately either side of the greenhouse. If you set up your benching so the legs are placed (but not fixed) in e.g. concrete sockets, it can be taken down as necessary. The resulting space can be used to plant out cucumbers or tomatoes in summer, or to see container-grown plants safely through the winter. However, heavy concrete benches aren't suitable — they're almost impossible to move! Lightweight, movable aluminium benches are easy to erect and widely available. It's important for the legs to stand on a hard surface.

Hanging shelves are hung from the roof structure. Since they provide another working surface, they help to make better use of space in the greenhouse. Hanging shelves are sheets of glass, plastic or wood supported by wires or angled aluminium strips.

Obviously hanging units put a strain on the greenhouse structure, so don't try to mount them in a lightweight polythene tunnel. If you're not sure that your greenhouse has the necessary load-bearing capacity, check with the manufacturers.

It's always an advantage to have a propagation bed if you're rooting cuttings or growing plants from seed. In a warm greenhouse it's a necessity if you want to exploit the full range of possibilities available to you. In a temperate greenhouse it's no waste of space to have a place set aside for for sowing, pricking-out and raising young plants. Delicate plant species can also be propagated here. The best arrangement is to use a small area of the benching fitted with electric soil warming cables to ensure that most of the heat goes upwards. Rigid polystyrene sheets can be used as a base under the electric cables. Similarly you can contain the heat inside your propagation bed by covering the top with glass or plastic sheeting, lifting this for ventilation as necessary.

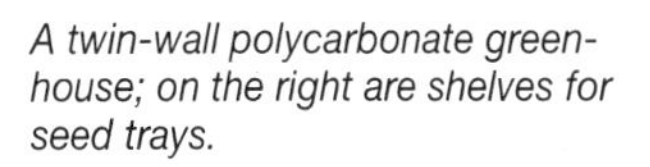

A twin-wall polycarbonate greenhouse; on the right are shelves for seed trays.

If it isn't possible to heat the greenhouse from your domestic central heating system, and the greenhouse hasn't got its own heating unit, soil warming becomes really useful. Most soil warming cables no operate on mains voltage, and are spaced out a few inches apart on the benching, usually with a 2-in (5-cm) layer of compost or sand over them. Another type of bench warming has heating cables encased in metal foil. These are available in specific sizes.

The more stable your greenhouse, the more solid your floor-covering should be. Concrete made and laid on the spot creates a durable surface. Concrete slabs, especially those with a roughened surface, look good and are very suitable, providing a non-slip surface to walk on. Be careful with smooth-finished concrete — it tends to be slippery when wet, and can easily lead to accidents!

Paths should be laid on a firm gravel substrate, or better still on concrete pads at the corners of the slabs. The path should be raised slightly above the borders

A commercial-type propagation bed, shown here with heating pipes, is ideal for striking cuttings, sowing seed and anything else that needs base heat.

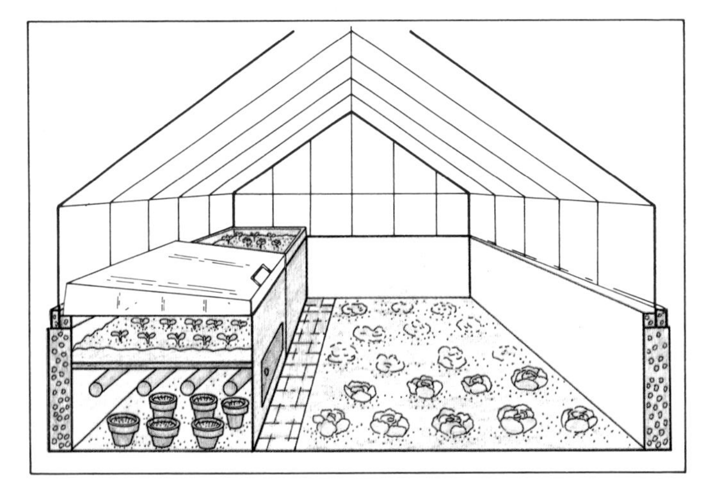

so it's easy to keep clean. Gravel and sand paths are rather a makeshift solution; constant toing and froing may serve to compact them, but they're very likely to get dirty and they're troublesome to clean. Besides, the crunching sound that accompanies your every step can get on your nerves — and you may have to put in edging strips to keep this kind of path at a higher level than the surrounding soil.

Wooden slats and duckboards, on the other hand, are an entirely suitable substitute for slabs. They're easy to move around, and if you want to resite your greenhouse — not uncommon with a polythene tunnel — you can use them again. A potting or work bench is a useful fitting in any greenhouse. If you've built a generously-sized greenhouse you can dedicate part of your benching (sited at some convenient location) to seed sowing, pricking out, potting on and other purposes.

Resourceful gardeners will also use movable staging; this can be mounted on the edges of the fixed benches to bridge the central path when you need an extra surface. Another good idea is to put a general-purpose bench at the far end of the greenhouse, above the path.

Greenhouse lighting is useful. Once it's fitted, you can take care of your plants in the evening or at night — or show them off to your visitors after dinner. Fit one or more lights: 3-6 W/m² of greenhouse area should be enough. For a 10 ft × 16 ft 6 in (3 × 5 m) greenhouse that will work out at 45-90 W — i.e. one 40, 60 or 100 W light bulb. However, you'll get better illumination if there are two light sources. The figure for fluorescent tubes is 2 W/m², so in our example greenhouse you'd need about 30 W. Use a 40 W tube — the lowest rating that's available. The colour you need is 'warm white'.

Ideally, your greenhouse should have a piped water supply. If it's a cool greenhouse, you're only going to need this in the summer. In winter you can turn it off at the mains. Container-grown plants, and any others that are overwintering in the greenhouse, will only need a modest amount of water. You can easily fetch this in a watering can from an indoor tap that isn't vulnerable to frost. A temperate greenhouse, on the other hand, needs a permanent water supply, and for a warm house it's absolutely essential. The pipes must be laid 32-40 in (80-100 cm) below ground to avoid any risk of frost damage; your water needs to be available all year round. If the greenhouse adjoins your home, it's a lot easier to solve this problem with a temporary hosepipe supply from spring to autumn.

You'll also need a tub or water butt for collecting water. Ideally you'll want to fill it with rainwater — that way you won't have to use drinking water for your plants. This can be a consideration when water's in short supply, especially if your supply is metered. Admittedly you won't collect very much from the greenhouse roof. However, perhaps the rainwater from your house is collected in an underground cistern. If so, you could pipe the runoff from your greenhouse there as well — and it shouldn't be a problem to get water back from the cistern to the greenhouse with the help of a small pump. Otherwise you could put a water butt next to the greenhouse and connect it to the gutter with a downpipe. If you cover the butt, this will minimise the growth of algae in the water.

A greenhouse path made from portable wooden slats.

Watering

Water doesn't just keep your plants in good shape, it also releases nutrients from the soil or compost. The amount of water you'll need depends on what you're growing. The rule of thumb is 240-275 gallons per sq yd (1300-1500 l/m^2) per year; in the cold frame it is 145-185 gallons (800-1000 l). Both are averages. While a single cucumber plant needs up to 110 gallons (600 l) in a single growing season, succulents manage on 145 gallons per sq yd (800 l/m^2) or even less, for a year. If your greenhouse is heated in winter, you must have a water supply readily available, and it must be frost-resistant. Have your water butt under the tap so stored water can reach greenhouse temperature before application.

Watering by hand

It's easy to scoop up water from the water butt with a watering can. For newly sown seeds and rooting cuttings, a half-gallon (two-litre) can with a fairly long spout and a fine rose is adequate. If you're watering pot plants or seedlings that are growing on, you can use a bigger can, say 1-2 gallons (4.5-9 l). Another possibility is to use a hose and spray nozzle, which isn't as damaging as it's sometimes made out to be.

Plastic-lined benching makes it easier to provide water. You'll need a level area of benching with a 1.5-2-in (4-5-cm) rim all round it. Line this shallow basin with 720-gauge polythene sheeting and fill it with a 1.2-in (3-cm) layer of chalk-free coarse sand (the grains should be about 2-3 mm in diameter). Level off the sand and push your pots into it. To ensure the water supply is evenly distributed you must stand all of them upright, and put them at the same depth in the sand. Now if you moisten the sand the compost in the pots will draw it up by capillary action. Take care when using clay and plastic pots together. Plastic pots retain the water much longer than clay ones.

Instead of sand you could lay capillary matting on the prepared benching. This soaks up water, which is then taken up by the pots and boxes placed on top of it. A new type of capillary matting (Fibertex) has a perforated black polythene cover. This largely avoids the growth of unsightly algae.

A seep hose offers a good solution to the problem of supplying water to a capillary mat. The hose has tiny holes along its entire length, through which water slowly seeps out. The bi-wall type, allowing for an even water flow, is the best.

Greenhouse shelves can also be fitted out with plastic and capillary matting and watered with drip tubing. You can even water individual plants drop by drop. This 'trickle irrigation' is achieved by laying a plastic tube down the middle of the benching. Thinner individual tubes branch off to the plant pots,

Workbench, tools, plants – what more could a gardener desire?

Left *A potentiometer for automatic water supply*
Centre *Seep hoses*
Right *Drippers for individual plants*

where they're held in place with pegs or small weights. Plants growing in the borders can be individually watered in the same way.

With a little care you can even build yourself an overhead spray kit consisting of a tube with spray nozzles screwed into it. It's ideal for seedlings that have been planted out, especially vegetables. Spray-line kits can be bought ready-to-use, which avoids complications.

Automatic watering

With a solenoid valve and a moisture sensor you can regulate the water supply to capillary matting or a sand tray completely automatically. The same system can be used for benching and shelves alike. This saves a great deal of work and controls the supply more precisely. Besides, an automatic system means that water for your plants will always be available when it's needed.

In a drip watering system, the water is fed drop by drop through thin tubes directly to the root area of the plant, seeping out under minimal pressure. This method of watering can reduce water demand by up to 50 per cent. The flow of water is regulated by sensors, or plant bugs, that expand when they become wet. Since the system responds actively to dryness and moisture, the plants are supplied only with the amount of water they actually need. It's especially good for plants that will suffer if their leaves get wet.

You can create a fully automated watering system using a water computer in conjunction with a moisture sensor. Automatic systems with a potentiometer switch give reliable results. The sensor is sited in the root area of the plant: the rest of the system includes supply tubes and drippers, control equipment, a solenoid valve, and a pressure reducer for connection to the mains water supply. A system like this is pricy, but it does get over the problem of 'unsupervised' days. You can automate an overhead spray system in much the same way by adding a solenoid valve, a moisture sensor and a controller.

If you're still a novice greenhouse gardener and want to get plants safely through the winter, you should take some basic rules of plant care to heart. Make sure the conditions you provide for your plants are appropriate to the time of year when light levels are low. This applies to watering, too. Water sparingly, providing no more than the plants actually need. If you douse the plants in water you may very well cause rot — at this time of year they'll hardly get a chance to dry off. In any case, the plants aren't growing as luxuriantly now as they were during the long, light days of summer.

Linked central heating

The best solution to the heating question may be to connect the greenhouse to a domestic central heating or off-peak electrical heating system. This is easy enough if your greenhouse is contiguous with house. If there's a gap between the house and the greenhouse it can sometimes be bridged. If you're planning this, talk to an experienced heating engineer. Remember that in many systems the boiler will be turned off at night.

Other systems

Hot-water heating

In this system, water heated in a boiler flows through metal pipes. If the greenhouse has permanent benching, some of the pipes can be laid underneath it to give base heat. Otherwise the pipes are laid along the side wallss in high greenhouses they can also be laid along the middle of the roof sections. Another factor determining their position is the layout of the interior fittings. Don't put heating pipes where plants could be damaged by them.

An **expansion tank** is fitted at the highest point of the pipework. This takes up the increase in the volume of water, which expands as it is heated.

If water is to be circulated by force of gravity, the pipes have to be laid with a slight slope of about 1 in per 100 in (1 per cent) of pipe away from the boiler. It's better to use a circulating pump, which makes the slope unnecessary.

A well-designed hot-water heating system guarantees that the entire growing space will be evenly heated. It's safe and reliable, but it does have a built-in time lag. It takes a considerable time for the water to heat up in the boiler and circulate through the pipes; conversely, once the system's been turned off it continues to produce heat for quite a while.

Electric heating

This is more suitable for heating in the transitional seasons of spring and autumn, and can easily be installed and connected by the amateur if the greenhouse already has a power supply. Electric heaters (usually fan heaters) aren't affected by ventilation; they can be fitted anywhere, and there's no need to store fuel for them. They are equipped with automatic thermostats which keep the temperature in the greenhouse at the level you have chosen. But the cost of electricity limits your scope for using them.

Tubular heaters can also be used to provide electric heating for greenhouses. Frost guards are used in places where frost is a threat (e.g. near water pipes). They can also be used to keep a greenhouse frost-free. The thermostat is set at a particular temperature (e.g. 41°F/5°C), and when the temperature drops below this, the heater turns itself on until the greenhouse temperature returns to 41°F (5°C).

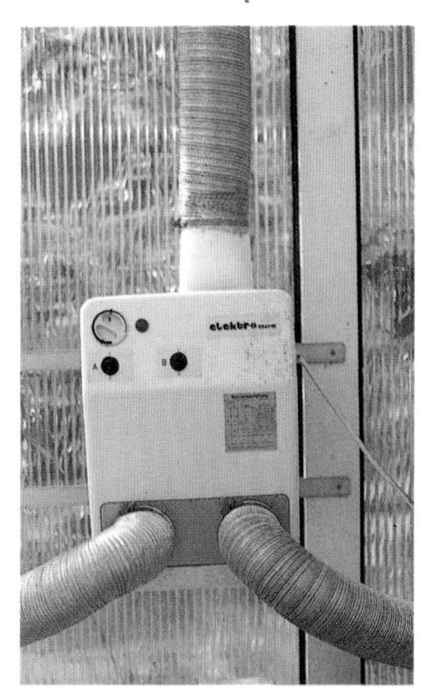

Above *A recirculated air heater with continously variable automatic control — designs vary.*

Left *A congenial conservatory atmosphere in the greenhouse.*

Air and fan heaters

These can be fuelled by oil or gas (though both types may need to be connected to a power point). The built-in fan expels the hot air. A thermostat allows you to maintain the temperature at the level you want.

Below *Gilled hot-water heating pipes used for transitional heating.*

Gas heating

Many gas boilers and heaters are specially designed to burn propane or Calor gas, but there are also the so-called 'universal' heaters that will burn either bottled gas or natural gas. With these you can start by using bottled gas, then switch to using natural gas once it's available; just get a pipe laid to the greenhouse when gas is laid to the house. Air for combustion is drawn from outside and vented back outside. Such heaters will normally feature spark ignition, a flame guard, and thermostatic temperature control.

Appliances that rely on small batteries rather than mains electricity are very useful if they need to be a long way away from the mains supply. Appliances which draw in air from the outside for combustion, and which vent the exhaust gases outside again through a chimney, should be run like solid-fuel stoves or oil-fuelled boilers.

Gas heaters with a balanced flue installed on an outside wall don't need a chimney. Exhaust gases are vented outside straight through the wall. These days they are widely used for home heating, and are very efficient. Some types of gas heater don't require a flue, but are best used for providing only low heat.

Liquid gas is stored in built-in tanks or, for smaller quantities, in bottles. There are regulations governing the storage of liquid gas: it's important, for your own safety, to follow them.

Space heating

Space heating warms the entire greenhouse. Methods include hot-water heating, convectors, fan heaters, and electric heaters. Electric heaters are expensive unless you use a storage type powered by off-peak electricity — difficult to control by day. Fan heaters use electricity and gas (or electricity alone) to heat air which is then blown into the greenhouse. Other heating appliances include:

Oil stoves

These can be vented, but this isn't usual. A supplementary fan above the stove can help to achieve good heat circulation and distribution. Another possible option is a solid-fuel stove, but it's labour-intensive, and far from being an ideal solution to the heating problem. In any case, it has an undesirable impact on the environment.

Propane gas heaters are economical in use, need no chimney and can be thermostatically controlled.

Moveable heaters

Infra-red heating doesn't have to be permanently installed, but provides heat at a wavelength that's easily absorbed by plant leaves. As well as plug-in heaters, there are bottled-gas heaters for greenhouses without mains electricity. These heaters are better suited to keeping the greenhouse frost-free during transitional periods than for use as regular winter heating.

Free-standing **paraffin heaters** are cheap to buy and reasonably cheap to run, but can cause problems with fume damage if used to excess. They are best sited centrally, and it's a good idea to leave some ventilation open to disperse the fumes.

Many greenhouse gardeners use small paraffin stoves and paraffin lamps to keep greenhouses frost-free. Even tallow candles (the kind designed for food-warming stands) are used; you can put them underneath clay flower pots so that the warmth from these heated pots keeps the greenhouse frost-free. But this is nothing more than a makeshift form of heating. It helps to stop temperatures falling below freezing point, but it's best not to use it for a high level of heating. For the best results you should also use protective sheeting or fleece laid over the plants. You might also want to line the greenhouse with bubble polythene.

Soil warming

Soil or border warming keeps the 'feet' warm and the 'head' cool — a desirable combination for any plant (and any gardener). Used as supplementary heating in the propagation bed, it promotes root growth and seed germination. Here, too, you can use a hot-water heating system: for instance, you can take a long, winding tube off the main heating pipes and fit it with a stop valve.

In many commercial nurseries, propagation beds on the tops of benches are warmed with plastic pipes made from polythene. They're laid in the greenhouse border 10 in (25 cm) apart at a depth of 10 in (25 cm). The water is normally only about 20°F (11°C) hotter than the intended soil temperature. Soil heating systems are run with the water at 100–120°F (40–50°C).

In amateur circles, electricity is normally used for both soil and bench warming. There are two systems in common use for electric soil heating: heating cables, and heated wire foil. Heating cables are laid about 8 in (20 cm) deep and 12 in (30 cm) apart to warm the soil. The plastic-covered cables have a surface temperature of 85–100°F (30–40°C), and you simply plug them into the mains socket. A sensor pushed into the soil and connected to a thermostat keeps the soil temperature at your chosen level. These days both cable and mesh foil systems use mains voltages and are made up in specific sizes for various loadings.

Mains voltage electric cable heating is ideal for soil or bench warming.

Local heating

Large-diameter plastic solar pipes store heat during the day and release it to warm the plants and the ground during the night.

For the serious gardener, heating the root area of plants can be far more effective than heating the greenhouse as a whole. This type of heating involves transmitting warmth from steel or plastic pipes laid directly beside the plants. Water flows through these pipes at a temperature of about 120°F (50°C).

This makes better use of the heat and saves energy. Under optimal conditions, you can save up to 30 per cent of your heating costs compared with space heating. The heat has a direct effect on the plants and influences the microclimate. It helps to remove damp, to warm the soil, to renew the air (because warm air rises), and to ensure that plants dry off rapidly after watering.

The pipes are arranged so that every row of plants in the border or on the benching gets localised warmth from one side. Flexible (or rigid) plastic pipes can be used, but steel pipes are more usual in commercial applications. The pipes will expand slightly when heated, and you may need to allow for this. Steel gilled pipes can give off four to five times more heat than plain piping because they have a larger surface area.

For localised heating you'll need the following equipment to ensure that your chosen temperature is maintained: a three-way mixer, a pump to circulate the water through the narrow 0.75-in (20-mm) pipes, and (ideally) a thermostatically controlled device to control tube and ambient temperatures. Above all you should have separate thermometers for the outward and return pipes. The difference between the two should not exceed 5-9°F (3-5°C). If you want this kind of heating system you should consult a qualified heating engineer.

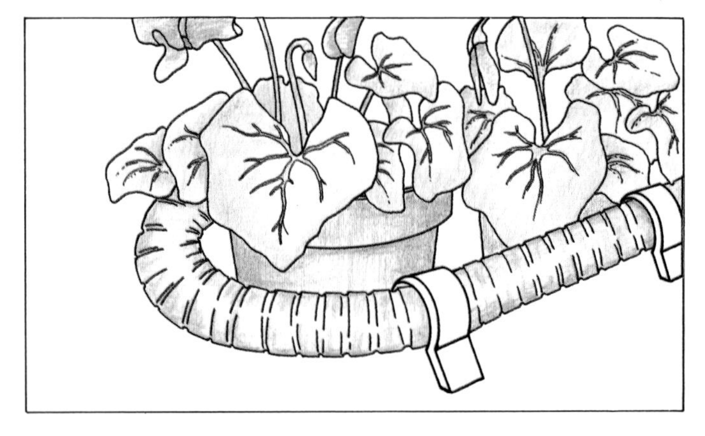

Localised heating pipes transfer warmth from the hot water flowing through them to the plants.

About heating

Heat consumption

In a greenhouse, different designs, construction materials and building types all have an effect on energy consumption. So does the actual rise in temperature that is required. A warm greenhouse needs more powerful heating equipment than a temperate or cool one. This is evident if we take as examples a warm house, which is to be kept at a night-time temperature of 63-65°F (17-18°C) and a daytime temperature of 75-79°F (24-26°C), and a frost-free greenhouse for over-wintering plants, which only needs to be kept in the range 32-41°F (0-5°C) day and night.

When the outside temperature is lower than that inside the greenhouse, heat will be lost through the external surfaces, and of course through any gaps where the greenhouse is not completely weathertight. The heat lost must be fully replaced by the heating system.

The extent of this heat loss depends on a number of factors. It depends on the difference between the temperature inside the greenhouse and that of its surroundings, and on the weather. When you are working out what the capacity of your heating system needs to be, you should take into account the maximum heat output that you are going to need. This is the amount of heat required when there is the largest possible difference between the temperatures inside and outside the greenhouse. You'll also need to take account of the external surface area of the greenhouse in your calculation.

Another important factor is the **thermal transmittance** (or thermal transmission) **coefficient** of the building materials, also known as the **U value** (or the **μ value**). The U value of a building material refers to the amount of heat, measured in British thermal units (Btu), which passes through one square foot of the material in one hour when there is a temperature difference between the inside and the outside of the material of one Fahrenheit degree. U values are thus expressed in Btu/sq ft/h/F°. The lower the U value, the better the material guards against heat loss.

Today U values are often expressed in metric units, where the U value represents the heat flow (power) in watts passing through one square metre of the material, with a difference in temperature of one centigrade degree between the inside and the outside. The metric unit of U value is thus W/m²/C° or W/m²/K, where K is the kelvin, the official scientific name for the centigrade degree.

To give an example, a pane of single glass 3 mm thick has a U value of 5.8 W/m²/K. By contrast, a perspex polycarbonate 16 mm thick has a U value of 2.9 W/m²/K — half as much heat loss as from the glass.

Any gaps in the greenhouse (e.g. at ventilators, doors etc.), any bridges for the cold created by parts of the frame, the prevailing weather conditions and so on can't really be calculated. All that sort of thing is indicated by the correction factor symbol U´ (U-prime). A typical **correction factor** might be about 20-30 per cent. Now you can work out how much heat is used, and thus how much heating capacity is needed overall. Expressed simply, you multiply the external area of the greenhouse by the difference in temperature between the inside and the outside of the greenhouse and by the U value, then apply the correction factor U´.

Let's take a theoretical example. On the basis of an internal temperature of +15°C and an external temperature of -15°C, 9.5 kW is needed. Applying the correction factor U´, it would be a good idea to have a heat source that can deliver around 11.6 kW.

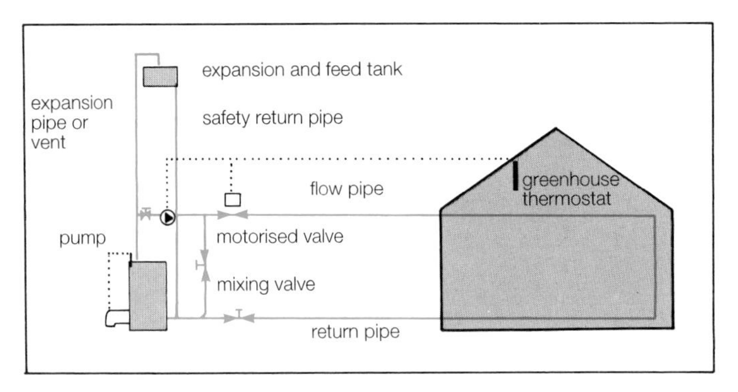

Diagram of a heating system and controls: oil-fired boiler with heating pump and motorised/mixing valves; flow and return runs; expansion vent and feed pipe, expansion and feed tank.

The source of heat

In many cases it's out of the question to install a heating system with a boiler because of the costs involved. But if it is an appropriate solution it's best to site the boiler in an anteroom, at a somewhat lower level. This room could also be equipped with a workbench or potting bench. When you're installing a hot-water heating system in a small greenhouse, it's a good idea to seek guidance from a professional heating engineer who can also take care of the fitting. Long-established firms that specialise in this type of work will also guarantee that your system operates without any problems.

It's cheaper to install and run oil or paraffin stoves, or gas or electric heaters, so these are the most popular choices. Even so, a good long-term solution for the serious gardener is still to connect the greenhouse to your domestic heating system. Obviously you'll have to adjust the boiler to a higher output setting so it can match the heating requirements of the greenhouse; and of course, the greenhouse system should be controlled independently of the system for the house.

A maximum–minimum thermometer shows the lowest overnight temperature the next morning; the highest daytime temperature can be read in the late evening.

Alarm

For a stock of valuable plants, an alarm is a wise investment. It gives an audible warning of any sudden breakdown in the heating system. It must run independently of mains electricity (i.e. battery-powered) in case of power cuts.

Thermometer

You need to be able to measure the temperature. If you hang several thermometers at different heights inside your greenhouse you will find that the temperature at ground level is several degrees cooler, because heat rises; yet it is often at lower levels that the most heat is needed. This is why a soil or localised heating system is so effective. To measure soil temperatures you need a special soil thermometer. It's important to be able to check the temperature where cuttings are being rooted, in seed trays and in the soil. You may also find that from autumn to spring the ground at the centre of a heated greenhouse is warmer than that at the sides. The only exception is in a greenhouse on solid, well-insulated foundations that protect it against cold from outside.

Ordinary thermometers can only show the temperature at a given moment: they cannot show whether it is being maintained. This is why a **maximum–minimum thermometer** can be so valuable. It allows you to read the lowest overnight temperature the following morning, and the highest daytime temperature late in the evening.

A 3mm-thick layer of rust on a boiler increases fuel consumption in a heating system by 25 per cent, so the boiler should occasionally be cleaned. A 'clean' heating system gives the best guarantee of trouble-free performance.

Always ensure that the air inlet is clear and unobstructed. If there isn't enough air the heating system will not work properly, and could become dangerous.

It's important to have a service contract with your heating engineers, and to keep their telephone number handy, though it's often possible to sort out minor faults yourself.

Saving energy

To reduce your energy consumption (and your heating costs), you should ensure that there is nowhere in or on the greenhouse where energy can be lost. If you have a hot-water pipe heating system, even the out and return pipes must be insulated. A 2-inch-diameter pipe gives off enough energy per hour per yard to heat half a square yard of greenhouse area to the temperate level for the same length of time. So insulate thoroughly, using at least a one-inch (30-mm) thickness of, for example, split tube foam pipe lagging. As a rule of thumb, the insulation should be as thick as the diameter of the pipe. After all, a thicker layer of insulation costs very little more, and the work involved in fitting it is minimal.

The boiler should be cleaned regularly; this saves 10-15 per cent of the heating costs on average over the year.

There are many things you can do to insulate the greenhouse, and a combination of methods will give better results. If you've fitted shading blinds, you could make energy savings of 20 per cent by drawing them down at night. Special thermal screens can make savings of 35 per cent. Sheets of white polystyrene 1.5-2 in (4-5 cm) thick fixed on the north side (or a gable end if your greenhouse is orientated north-south) are a great help; they can help you save from 40-50 per cent of your heating costs, though you will lose a little light. If your side walls don't have to be translucent (e.g. if you're not

With dry glazing, the aluminium glazing bar can be covered by a plastic cap.

growing plants under the benching) these too can be fitted with polystyrene to about the height of the benching.

When you're planning to save energy, don't forget the base, especially if you live in one of the colder parts of the British Isles. Here polystyrene foam (from a builders' merchant) or sheets of expanded polystyrene are better than polystyrene sheet, because they don't create problems with damp. They have a closed-celled structure with a sealed smooth surface, so they can't absorb moisture. They're also available with tongued and grooved edges, so sheets can be slotted tightly together to provide effective insulation.

You can save up to 10 per cent of energy consumption by painting the heating pipes with aluminium paint where they face the glazing, or by sticking strips of aluminium foil onto them. This will reduce the amount of heat that can radiate from the treated surfaces. To make sure the greenhouse itself gets enough heat, paint the inward-facing surfaces of your heating pipes with matt paint.

If you cover steel glazing bars with special adhesive strips you can reduce the flow of heat from the inside out. The energy saving is around 6 per cent.

Glass readily transmits short-wave radiation from the sun, and thus effectively traps the reflected long-wave radiation. In general, though, glass is a poor insulator, and you must allow for this when calculating heat loss and designing a heating system to cope with it. When designing or planning a greenhouse heating system it's usual to add 20–30 per cent extra heating capacity to cope with 'inadvertent' heat losses through various gaps.

If you use bubble plastic to line the inside of a greenhouse, you can achieve an energy saving of 30 per cent at relatively low cost. It's important to fix it so there aren't any gaps — but don't restrict the ventilation.

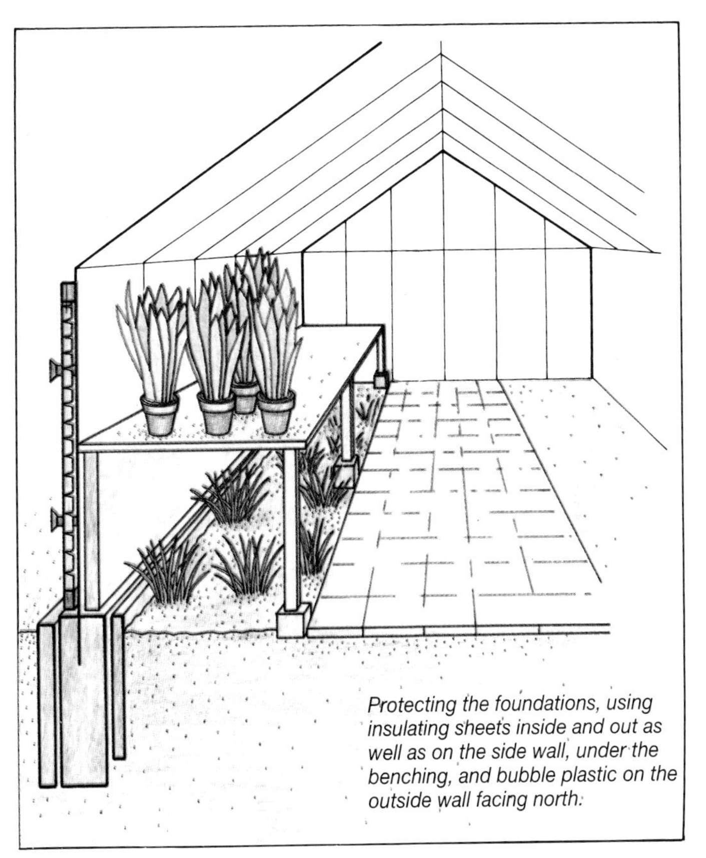

Protecting the foundations, using insulating sheets inside and out as well as on the side wall, under the benching, and bubble plastic on the outside wall facing north.

Double glazing is a permanent fixture — a double layer of glass — which can produce savings of around 35-40 per cent. But it is double the weight of single glazing, and needs a very solidly built greenhouse frame to support it.

If you're buying a greenhouse, ask if the framework is strong enough to make double glazing a feasible alternative. When you need to heat the greenhouse, you can attach hollow-chambered sheets of polycarbonate or Perspex with special fittings; they serve as supplementary insulation for the walls.

You can buy bubble plastic in various widths and lengths. The most effective insulator is the three-layered type with bubbles 1 inch (30 mm) in diameter. If it is unaffected by ultra-violet light it will last about three years when it's fixed to the inside of the greenhouse. Although it does provide insulation, there are disadvantages: for one thing, light levels inside will be reduced, partly as a result of water condensing on the inner side of the greenhouse glazing. Depending on the materials you could lose between 10-15 per cent of the light coming in.

With double glazing, the temperature on the inner side of the glass will be higher than with single glazing, so the humidity is higher, too. A well-insulated greenhouse is very weathertight, which means that air is exchanged far more slowly. The humidity is about 10 per cent higher, particularly at night, and this can lead to fungal diseases. Try to compensate by modifying your cultivation methods; give water exactly where it is needed, and in exactly the right amounts, e.g. by using drip tubing.

To get an accurate figure, work out how much energy will still be needed after each energy-saving step has been taken. Deduct the percentage of energy saved by the next step from that figure. As an example, consider an insulating method that produces a saving of 25 per cent. This means that only 75 per cent of the original energy input is still needed. A second measure yields, for example, 6 per cent: this, of course, is 6 per cent of the remaining 75 per cent, which is only 4.5 per cent of the original amount. So the energy requirement is still 70.5 per cent of the original amount, not 69 per cent!

The greenhouse climate, natural and artificial

In the greenhouse, the plants live in a completely different environment from that of the garden outside. Greenhouse plants don't get any water naturally, but they do have plenty of warmth available in summer — warmth which has to be supplied artificially in winter. And the amount of natural light available varies. The plants will grow best when the different factors — such as light, air, heat and humidity — are well balanced with one another.

Light

Plants can only produce organic substances from inorganic materials when light of sufficient intensity is available; they do this by the process of **photosynthesis**. When enough light is available it will promote the growth of strong and healthy plants, and has a positive effect on flower and fruit formation. Low light levels, particularly if combined with excessive heat, produce leggy, weak plants that are prone to infections. But there's a difference between plants that need diffused light conditions (e.g. tropical plants) and others, such as cacti and succulents, that aren't greatly affected by direct sunlight.

Natural irradiation and protection from light

Because natural irradiation by sunlight is so important for the growth of plants, the site you have chosen for the greenhouse is also very significant. A site that's lightly shaded by trees and buildings offers definite advantages for some plant species. Others wouldn't be able to develop fully under these conditions. In most cases there won't actually be much scope for choice. There are limitations imposed by garden boundaries, surrounding buildings and the position of your house, especially since you also need to work out how you're going to connect heating and water supplies to the greenhouse. Natural light is always available, and between spring and autumn there's often more than you really want: the more sunlight you have shining into the greenhouse, the hotter it gets inside. The gardener must often intervene to prevent damage from strong sunshine — for instance, by installing fabric blinds on tracks under the greenhouse roof. Some of these blinds can also be closed at night and used as insulation to help reduce heating costs.

The use of blinds reduces the effect of the sun's rays, and moderates their effect on temperature at the same time.

Shading blinds can also help to save energy if they are drawn at night

Plants need as much sun as possible at the time of year when light levels are low. Dirty roofs and walls restrict the amount of light passing through quite considerably. Clean all panes of glass (or other material) regularly, so they're always sparkling clean. At the same time you can replace any broken panes promptly and deal with any gaps in the structure.

Blinds can be fitted both inside and outside the greenhouse. External blinds are more expensive and more complicated, but have the advantage of stopping the radiation before it even reaches the roof.

The cheapest solution is to apply a shading wash, using a sort of whitewash. However, this produces permanent shading, which reduces light even in dull weather. Flour-and-water mixtures have the advantage that they will become transparent in the rain, so they won't limit lighting in this way. A product called Varishade is also very useful.

In the winter months light levels are low, and this lack of light is the chief factor limiting plant growth. You can alleviate the problem by using supplementary lighting.

Exterior shading is technically complicated but very effective.

Supplementary lighting

In the winter the sun, source of all natural light, is working at a greatly reduced level. This means that lighting conditions for greenhouse plants are often less than ideal. At midday in summer, sunlight can provide as much as 100,000 lux; in winter this figure might fall to as low as 1,000 lux.

Light is indispensable for growth. If light levels fall very low, the development of the plant will be disrupted to a considerable degree. This is why supplementary lighting can be useful, especially at the time of year when natural light is hard to come by.

Daylight simulation lighting promotes growth, helping photosynthesis by replacing energy that's no longer available from sunlight. With this type of lighting, plants can be grown even at the darkest time of year — at a price! Special moisture-proof luminaires are used, and should be hung around 18-30 in (45-75 cm) above the plants. It's a good idea to have some way of moving them up and down (e.g. by hanging them on chains) so you can change raise them as the plants grow taller. It's important to ensure that the whole area is evenly lit. If you're raising seedlings, daylight simulation speeds up their growth rate, and allows you to use your greenhouse more intensively.

If you want to raise plants when the days are short, you'll need supplementary lighting.

Terminology

Lamps are the light sources; **luminaires** (or **fixtures**) are holders for lamps, and may or may not be fitted with a reflector. **Luminous flux** is the intensity of radiation emitted from a light source independent of the direction in which it is radiated; it is measured in lumen (lm). The **illuminance**, which

is expressed in lux (lx), is a measure of the amount of light (the luminous flux, measured in lumen) that falls on a surface one metre square. Thus 1 lux = 1 lumen/m^2.

The **luminous efficacy** (or **overall luminous efficiency**) is a measure of the performance of a light source. It expresses the luminous flux produced by an input of 1 watt of electrical energy, and is measured in lumen/watt (lm/W). The higher the lumen/watt ratio, the more economical the light source. The **radiation efficacy** indicates the total electromagnetic radiation that is produced per watt of electricity consumed. It's measured in milliwatts per watt (mW/W; cf. luminous efficacy). This information can be useful when you know the spectral energy distribution of a given type of lamp.

There are complete sets of lights available to simulate and supplement daylight for groups of plants, if you don't plan on illuminating the entire growing area.

Incandescent lamps have a high luminous flux in the infra-red region, so they can't possibly be used for daylight simulation. The large red component of their light would make all the plants grow excessively tall. Besides, their luminous efficacy is only 5-7 per cent of the electrical energy used. Fluorescent lamps come quite close to the ideal for lighting. The radiation efficacy, at 200 mW/W, is high. They don't produce much heat, and they last a long time (about 10,000 hours).

Cymbidium hybrid 'Heritage'

Meanwhile, ready-to-use lighting sets are widely available; you simply have to hang them up. Bear in mind, however, that the illuminance (measured in lux) decreases the farther they are from the surface to be lit. Specialist plant lights are available in garden centres; be sure to hang them at the recommended height.

Plants from tropical regions shouldn't be lit for longer than twelve hours a day (daylight plus artificial light). Plants from our latitudes can be lit for a total of 12-16 hours.

If you're looking for lamps to supplement daylight, it's worth considering 3- or 5-gang fluorescent lamps. (They're rated at 18-25 W, and the colour is 'warm white de luxe'.) You should hang them about 12-20 in (30-50 cm) above the plants. Compact fluorescent lamps have proved useful for lighting smaller areas; the colour you want is 'warm white'.

Other types of lamp include high-pressure mercury vapour lamps and high-pressure metal-halide vapour lamps (from 35 W; the luminous efficacy is rather low, but the visual effect is pleasing). High-pressure sodium vapour lamps are also available as complete sets, and are among the types that make the most efficient use of energy. This is why commercial growers so often use them.

Ventilation

If you're raising young plants you'll need a good supply of air. The growing seedlings must be hardened off gradually, so they can get used to conditions outside the greenhouse. Many other plants, particularly warm houseplants, need a less generous air supply.

Air supply and heating really need to be considered together, since ventilation is used to control excessive heat in the greenhouse. All styles of greenhouse (however they've been built) and all types from the cool to the warm house need fittings for ventilation. They're necessary to draw in fresh air, to release used, warm air, and to reduce humidity with many types of crop. Actually there can't be too many vents in a greenhouse. It's better to find that you're always leaving one of them shut than to have a greenhouse that gets too hot because there aren't enough of them.

It's often said that a warm house doesn't need as much ventilation as other types. This is very far from the truth. If your warm house is also being used to raise seedlings, you'll still need a generous supply of air.

The need for really good ventilation becomes even clearer if you look at what can happen in winter. If there's a temperature difference of 54°F (30°C) between inside and outside, you'll have to arrange for some 290 W/sq yd (350 W/m^2) of heating to maintain the temperature inside. In a perfect world all greenhouses would be equally well-equipped with ventilators to make them suitable for all the possible uses one might make of them. After all, who can predict exactly how they will be using their greenhouse today, tomorrow or many years from now?

Left *Automatic vents regulate the flow of air to achieve a pre-set temperature.*

Small polythene tunnels can easily be ventilated without the need for automation.

Below *This continuous run of vents in the greenhouse roof enables the best possible climatic conditions to be achieved.*

The important thing is to have plenty of *potential* ventilation, even if you don't use it all. It should be possible to achieve any gardening objective, whether you're raising seedlings, growing cucumbers (which doesn't need much ventilation), growing lettuce and tomatoes (which need a good supply of air) or using your greenhouse to overwinter plants.

Heat

In winter, heating replaces the natural warmth that is no longer available from solar radiation. In a greenhouse it's possible to ensure an even temperature. However, even winter sunshine can sometimes make the greenhouse too hot. The answer is to regulate your heating system with a thermostat, so that sunshine doesn't raise the temperature too high.

In a warm house with a hot-water heating system, you can keep the greenhouse temperature at 75°F (24°C) even during a cold winter, though it's likely to be expensive. The heating pipes are laid under the benching, and in various other positions around the greenhouse. Hot water is drawn from the domestic system or from a dedicated boiler, which can be housed in a small potting shed. The warm house can also have a propagation bed with hot-water or electric heating.

The temperate house needs fewer pipes, and in some circumstances it may also be possible to use an oil or gas stove for heating. At very least you should have an electrically heated propagation bench so there's enough ground warmth inside the greenhouse to raise plants. If you are growing plants in the greenhouse borders you could install a soil heating system.

A cool house will have a little heating if it's used for overwintering plants — an oil stove can provide what's needed. Electric fan heaters often make adequate frost protectors, and help to prolong the growing season in spring and autumn. Even paraffin lamps can be used as makeshift heat sources. But a cool house needn't stay cool for ever; with more heating you can even turn it into a warm house, as long as it's a well-built structure.

Humidity

Air humidity is measured with a **hygrometer**. If the air is completely saturated, it is said to have 100-per-cent relative humidity. This is the maximum amount of water vapour that can be absorbed into the air before water droplets begin to form.

It is as important to know about humidity levels, and the best humidity range for your plants, as it is to know about their temperature requirements. Lettuce, for example, grows best when relative humidity is between 65 and 80 per cent.

Temperature and humidity should be kept in balance with one another. The humidity should be about twice, or at the most three times, as high as the temperature in degrees Celsius. (Alas, this rule of thumb cannot be used with Fahrenheit temperatures.) To calculate the appropriate humidity when there is strong sunshine, add 8C° to the measured temperature; in moderate sunshine add 4C°. For example, a measured temperature of 18°C plus 4C° = 22°C; the target relative humidity is therefore 44-66 per cent. You can reduce the humidity by ventilation and by raising the air temperature.

Humidity can be increased by spraying water. But if you are very fastidious and your plants require high humidity, you'll hardly be able to create an appropriate climate for them just by spraying the greenhouse path; it's much better to use an electronically controlled misting system, which raises humidity levels automatically. Increasing the humidity will also have the effect of reducing the temperature, because heat is taken up by evaporation.

In a cool greenhouse, there will certainly be no need for a misting system. With double glazing the inner pane is warmer, which leads to higher humidity and less evaporation.

For many plants from the tropics, humidity is essential to life. In this greenhouse a misting system provides humidity.

Managing the climate

If you had to control every aspect of the greenhouse climate yourself, at exactly the right time, you'd be in there all day turning on the heating (or turning it down), adjusting the humidity at the critical moment, opening and shutting vents — in short, tailoring the climate (and every other factor affecting growth) to suit the plants precisely.

Of course, keeping all these factors perfectly balanced won't provide everything that your plants are going to need. Even so, air, light, heat and humidity form the basic framework. When all these elements are in harmony, even beginners won't find it difficult to succeed.

If you've fitted supplementary lighting, you'll need a time switch to turn it on and off. A light-sensitive switch is also useful; this turns on the lighting when the available daylight falls below a certain level. A combination of light-sensitive and time switches can be particularly effective. The light-sensitive switch turns the system on, and the time switch turns it off at the pre-set time.

Air supply, too, can be regulated automatically. Once set, non-electric vent openers will provide your chosen level of ventilation with no further effort on your part. This is also possible with 'forced ventilation', using extractor fans.

An automatic control system providing measured amounts of heating is equally necessary, and means that your greenhouse won't need constant attention in winter, either. Special equipment is available to reduce night-time temperatures. The plants tolerate this very well, and it helps to save fuel costs.

Moisture supply, too, can easily be regulated. It's a real help to have the water supply to your watering system controlled by moisture sensors, which deliver water to the plants as they need it. You can achieve precise control of humidity with adjustable electronic mist systems fitted with **hygrostats** (automatic humidity regulators). The relative humidity can be set anywhere between 20 and (virtually) 100 per cent, so the system is equipped to meet the demands of any plant.

Under the right climatic conditions, it's possible to create the effect of a tropical forest in your greenhouse.

Soil

This is the place where the roots can take hold, and the source of nutrients for your plants. The ideal to aim for is a friable, well-structured soil, rich in humus, with good drainage and optimum air porosity. Fertile soil can be recognised by the rich, active life it contains.

Greenhouse soil must often support vegetables that are growing quickly during a large part of the year, so it has to meet far greater demands than garden soil. Plants thrive in what is usually an ideal climate, and higher ground temperatures speed up the succession of plants. Organic substances are used and broken down more quickly, so the humus content decreases as a result of harvesting and the processes of biological decomposition. To keep up soil fertility an optimum **supply of humus** is very important. Well-rotted horse manure is ideal; dig in about 9 lb/sq yd (5 kg/m^2), especially before you plant cucumbers, tomatoes and peppers. Compost and peat substitutes (e.g. bark humus from composted tree bark) can also be worked in; they improve the structure of the soil.

The pH value establishes the acidity of the soil and indicates its lime content. The range goes from very acid (pH under 4.5) to alkaline (pH over 7.4; no need of lime). Vegetables do best with values between 6 and 7. You can measure the pH value with indicator strips available from gardening suppliers.

It's worth having a soil analysis done at a laboratory. A routine check every 3-4 years will tell you about the type of soil, its phosphate and potassium content, and its pH, including any need for lime. To collect the sample, take soil specimens at a depth of 8-10 in (20-25 cm) from several places and mix them together thoroughly. The results of the laboratory check will help you to match your supply of nutrients to the real needs of your plants, and to avoid excessive use of fertilisers. Alternatively you can buy a soil-testing kit from your garden centre.

Older books suggest that you should give your greenhouse soil an annual soaking with water. This is intended to wash unused fertiliser out into the subsoil, which avoids a build-up of excess salts. Given the burden this places on the environment, it's no longer really possible to justify such a procedure.

A good supply of humus is essential to keep the border soil in fertile condition.

Composts and growing mediums

This is what a good compost should be like: light, loose-structured and good at taking up and retaining moisture.

Among other qualities, composts and growing mediums should retain water well and deliver it to the plants gradually; they should have a loose structure, with a low weight relative to volume; they should provide an adequate store of nutrients, releasing them gradually; and their pH should be appropriate to their intended use. Composts and growing mediums are needed for raising plants in seed trays, and later for pricking out and possibly for growing on in pots.

Mixing your own composts

If you don't want to buy ready-prepared mediums, you have access to a supply of well-rotted garden compost, and you enjoy experimenting, you can put together your own compost mix. A good general mix is 30 per cent each of garden compost, bark humus and garden soil plus 10 per cent sand.

Use mixes of garden soil, compost and sand in the proportions 4:4:1 for plants in the greenhouse border. Add peat or bark humus for seed and potting composts. These days it is regarded as good environmental practice to use less peat and to concentrate on peat substitutes such as coir (granulated coconut pith), timber and brewery waste. However, their value and use are still being tested.

You can buy various products to improve the texture, porosity and water-holding capacity of both home-made and proprietary growing media and composts. The most common are Perlite (expanded volcanic lava) and Vermiculite (expanded mica), though other products such as ground-up plastic are also used to improve texture.

There are various ways of adding specific organic or inorganic fertilisers to increase the nutrient level of compost. The most popular approach is to use a 'slow release' or 'complete' fertiliser mixture such as Osmocal, Chempak or Vitax Q4, at recommended rates. Some of these products (e.g. Chempak) include lime, and most aim to release their nutrients over a period.

However, commercially prepared composts are safer and more consistent in their nutrient content and their structure. Above all, there is no risk that they will contain weed seeds and potential sources of infection, both of which are possible in garden compost. There are many ready-made brands (e.g. Fisons, Levingtons etc.) based on peat and sold for specific purposes such as seed sowing and potting.

The John Innes soil-based composts have recently had a new lease of life, as environmentally minded gardeners are increasingly concerned about excessive use of peat. Choose a brand that carries the JIMA (John Innes Manufacturers' Association) logo.

Fertilisers

When a sequence of crops is well organised, nutrients that are being used up must be supplemented by properly-targeted fertilisers. An excess of mineral and organic nutrients damages the plants and the environment. This excess passes unused into the groundwater, where it contributes to the accumulation of pollutants (including nitrates) and endangers the drinking water supply. Nitrates in the soil are very mobile. It's essential to test the soil so you can work out what's actually needed: a shortage of nitrates will weaken the plants and make them vulnerable to pests and diseases.

Organic manures and fertilisers include horse manure (also available dried as granules), garden compost, green manures (where growing plants are cut and dug in), dried blood and bone meal, as well as compounds with organic bases. These have a gradual and long-lasting effect. While the simple organic fertilisers (such as hoof and horn) usually contain very little potassium, the compound products and dried horse manure have a better balance of nutrients — and they work faster, too.

There are many types of organic fertiliser on the market with varying nutrient content. They tend to be more expensive than chemical and inorganic types, but many gardeners prefer them on environmental

Fertilisers for vegetables

Strong feeders (tomatoes, cucumbers, melons, aubergines, peppers, pumpkins)	Before planting, work in generous amounts of compost and/or well-rotted horse manure; depending on the nutrient content of the soil, apply up to 3.5 oz/sq yd (120 g/m²) of organic-mineral or 1.5 oz/sq yd (50 g/m²) of complete fertiliser. Monthly follow-on applications of liquid fertiliser at recommended rates; for kohl rabi top-dressing with 0.5 oz/sq yd (20 g/m²).	Before planting, work in generous amounts of compost and/or well-rotted horse manure; add up to 5-6 oz/sq yd (180-200 g/m²) of organic compound as necessary. Apply a commercial organic liquid fertiliser as necessary, or mulch with more compost.
Moderate feeders (Chinese leaf, oriental radish, spinach, endives, onions, chives, climbing beans, kohl rabi)	Depending on what nutrients are present in the soil, apply up to 3 oz/sq yd (100 g/m²) of organic-mineral fertiliser, or half the quantity of complete fertiliser.	Before planting, work in compost and also apply up to 3.5 oz/sq yd (120 g/m²) of organic compound fertiliser. If necessary, follow on with compost or plant liquid fertiliser.
Minimal feeders (Lamb's lettuce, radish, parsley, dwarf beans, lettuce)	1.75-2.5 oz/sq yd (60-80 g/m²) of organic-mineral fertiliser or half the quantity of complete fertiliser.	Work in compost as necessary and/or up to 1.5-2 oz/sq yd (50-70 g/m²) of organic compound fertiliser.

With all fertilisers: depending on the nutrients they contain, follow the instructions provided!

Cucumbers need plenty of water and plenty of warmth, as well as measured applications of fertiliser.

grounds. They also have a longer-term action, and can improve soil structure. However, nitrates can leach into water supplies from both organic and inorganic sources.

Organic–mineral fertilisers are a mixture of organic materials and mineral salts. Many products are about 35 per cent organic.

Inorganic fertilisers are salts that are rapidly taken up by the plants and have a more immediate effect. There are many types on the market.

On open ground, water usually flows downward from above (except in hot weather). In the greenhouse it's often the other way round because the hot conditions produce intense surface evaporation. Inappropriate fertilising and watering can lead to a situation where water-soluble substances form a residue in the soil particles.

The result is damage caused by the excess salts, especially if the ground is short of humus. Visible symptoms include rolling of the leading shoots in tomatoes, and burn marks on cucumbers and lettuce. To avoid this problem you should deliver mineral fertilisers in several applications. Fertilise the ground before planting, and apply top-dressings later — but only as they are needed. If soil testing shows up a shortage of one particular nutrient, it's a good idea to apply the single missing substance rather than using a complete fertiliser.

By contrast, you're far less likely to have nitrate problems with organic fertilisers because their effects are slower and gentler. However, it's also impossible to calculate their effect in advance with the same precision: the results will depend on the activity of organisms in the soil and on other unpredictable factors. You will need to keep a careful eye on your plants. By way of compensation, organic fertilising maintains and improves the humus content of the soil in the longer term, producing healthy, abundant growth in your plants.

Mixed cultivation in an unheated polythene tunnel.

The nutrients

Nitrogen

This could be described as the driving force for growth. It's needed to build up protein, and for the development of the plant as a whole. It has a positive influence on the shoot and leaf formation of shoots and leaves; its effects are apparent immediately.

Deficiency: the leaves turn yellow, growth is poor and yield is reduced.

Excess: growth is lush, with a blue-green colour to the leaves; the tissues are soft, and the plant lacks structural strength.

Phosphorus

Affects the building up of cells, the formation and strengthening of roots and the formation of flowers, fruits and seeds.

Deficiency: small flowers, leaves reddish to browny-violet in colour. In well-fertilised soils, a phosphorus deficiency will hardly ever occur.

Potash

Necessary to form sugar, starch and protein. It ensures firm tissue and influences flavour and keeping qualities. Potash also increases resistance to frost, drought, pests and diseases.

Deficiency: reddish and yellow leaf edges.

Lime

Improves the structure of the soil, encourages soil life, acts as a soil improver, raises the pH-value and binds acid in the soil. The calcium it contains is a plant nutrient.

Magnesium

Affects green leaf formation.

Deficiency: rolling in of the leaf edges, lower leaves yellowish with green veins.

Trace elements

Iron, manganese, copper, zinc, molybdenum, sulphur, chlorine and boron have various functions, but in very small quantities all are essential to plant growth.

Hygiene and the protection of plants

Prevention is better than cure. If the climatic conditions are right, pests and diseases don't often get the chance to attack. Indiscriminate watering at night, for instance, can create high humidity that may result in botrytis disease (grey mould).

Increasingly, chemicals in the garden are a subject of public debate. If chemicals *are* to be used, you must use the exact concentrations specified and observe the full waiting time after applying them. Choose products that protect the environment; your choice must be appropriate for the location and for the growing season.

After some years of cultivation, you may need to **decontaminate the soil**. If so, steam treatment is appropriate. However, on a small scale this is only

really practical for growing mediums and composts. The best solution is resoiling, but if that involves digging out an area of 15 sq yd (15 m^2) to a depth of about 18 in (50 cm), then you'll have to shift 7.5 cu yd (7.5 m^3) of earth — twice!

Diseases and pests

Fungi and pests can attack both healthy and unhealthy plants, and any that are growing under less than ideal conditions will be vulnerable. If you repeatedly grow the same species of plant on the same patch of soil it may become 'sick', and this, too, will encourage pests and diseases.

Examine plants carefully, if necessary with a magnifying glass. If they have been attacked, take pot plants out of their pots and examine the root balls, checking the state of the root system. Healthy plants will usually have light-coloured, well-branched roots. Remove and destroy any affected parts of a plant at once — but remember that if the disease is well advanced there's little that can be done in the short term.

To raise healthy plants it's essential to use infection-free growing mediums and clean containers. You should also pay proper attention to the growing conditions (humidity, ventilation and temperature) and avoid draughts. Choose to grow plants whose needs conform with your existing crops, and which don't make for problems. Wherever possible, choose varieties that are resistant to such diseases as mildew, viruses, *fusarium* and root rot. Tomatoes, for instance, now have a lot of inbuilt resistance to disease.

Non-poisonous sticky **insect trap sheets** are invaluable. Another useful measure in the greenhouse is the **introduction of natural predators** of plant pests. Predatory mites, for instance, prey on red spider mites; ichneumon flies prey on whitefly, lacewings and gall midges, and ladybirds prey on aphids. The use of **nets** and **fleeces** helps to protect plants from vegetable flies.

A typical use of the greenhouse, with mature plants in the borders and others being raised on the staging.

Sticky yellow sheets are a well-tried method of dealing with whitefly without recourse to chemicals.

Waiting times for chemicals give the number of days which must elapse between applying the preparation and gathering the produce. They ensure that the active ingredients have been broken down by the time of harvest. Follow the manufacturer's instructions exactly when applying a preparation. If you use too much, you'll increase the waiting time; you may also leave larger residues, which can damage the plants.

Sowing seed

Don't start sowing too early: the short day length and low light intensity inhibit the rapid development of seedlings. It's better to buy the first batch of vegetable plants from a nursery or garden centre. But do consider raising later batches and summer flowers from seed. Sow the seed in February or March, depending on genus.

You can buy several different types of seed. **Normal seed** is largely free from impurities, but the seeds are not of uniform diameter. The packet will tell you whether or not it's been dressed. **Calibrated seed** has been sieved to ensure that all the seeds are a similar size; this can be helpful for plants such as radishes. In the case of **pelleted seed**, the individual seeds are coated with a clay to produce small balls of uniform size. The best pelleted seeds are **split pills**: the two halves of the 'pill' split, allowing the seed to emerge before it rots. They must be kept moist, and should not be sown more than about half an inch (1 cm) deep. With **seed tape** the seeds are attached at equal intervals along a narrow strip of paper which rots away. Lay the tape in the seed furrow half an inch (1 cm) deep, cover it, firm the soil and keep it moist. If you tend to sow your seeds too thickly, try seed tape, though the seeds can sometimes rot along with the tape.

Make your first sowings in trays, boxes or pots, using home-mixed or commercial seed compost. Most seeds should only be covered with a depth of compost equal to their own diameter. If you're not experienced, sow direct from the packet: tap it lightly to get the seed out into your container.

In the greenhouse you can raise many plants yourself, and make substantial savings.

Radish, spinach and lettuce don't need to be started in containers. Sow them direct into drills in the greenhouse border. Broadcast sowing can have unexpected disadvantages: getting rid of weeds later is a tricky business.

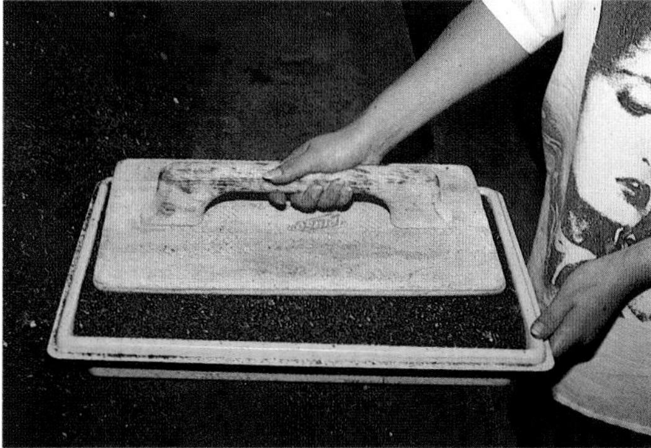

Left *Various possible ways of sowing seeds: sowing by hand (right), with seed tape (centre) and with a wheeled seed-sower (left).*

Centre and right *Don't sow too thickly. Firm down lightly and cover thinly with growing medium.*

Vegetative propagation

Taking cuttings

Tip cuttings use just the tips of shoots; for **stem cuttings**, stems or shoots are cut to roughly finger length. **Leaf cuttings** use only leaves, or parts of a leaf to propagate African violets, various succulents, begonia species and *Sansevieria* among others. Individual leaves are broken or cut and inserted into the propagation medium. New plants form on the underside of the leaf. Sets, air layering (see page 85), division, runners or grafting can all be successfully used for vegetative propagation.

When you're taking cuttings always ensure that your knife is sharp, your cut is smooth, and the plant tissue is not crushed. The cuttings are inserted in a mixture of loam, sand and peat, firmed in, watered and put in a glass-covered propagation bed. or in trays over heating cables. With base heat and a moist atmosphere the cuttings will root readily, though the time this takes will vary from plant to plant. The cuttings must not be allowed to wilt, so they'll need frequent spraying; keep them moist and warm but not too wet, or there's a chance they could rot. Mist propagating units can be useful here, though many people now prefer to cover the tray with a milky white polythene tent.

Cuttings should be kept in a light position out of direct sunlight. Once the roots have formed, reduce the humidity by increasing the ventilation.

Some plants root easily, and don't need any special treatments beforehand. They include tradescantias, *Pilea*, *Soleirolia* and *Selaginella*. They can be detached from the parent plant and put straight into their final containers.

Dividing plants

Some plant genera can easily be propagated by **division**. 'Making two from one' is a practical approach for plants with rhizomes (swollen underground stems). These include the well known *Sansevieria* (mother-in-law's tongue). Other plants such as *Spathiphyllum* (peace lily), some ferns, *Asparagus* and various others can also be propagated in this way. It's important to make sure that each section of the divided plant has enough roots.

Pricking out

Once the seedlings are past the seed-leaf stage, they should be **pricked out** (individually transplanted so they're farther apart). Prick them out into little pots: these can be individual cells within a modular system, single peat or clay pots, or the new generation of recyclable pots. If you put them into trays or pans, this will eventually mean disturbing the roots. In containers the plants have individual positions and can form root balls. When planted out, they can carry on growing undisturbed in their final positions. Put the containers somewhere light, e.g. on hanging shelves under the roof.

Potting up and potting on

No one who tries to raise their own plants can escape the stages of sowing, pricking out and potting up seedlings. Apart from the initial potting up, there can be even more to do by way of **potting on** — moving the plants from smaller to larger containers. Once the root ball is thick, almost matted, and consists almost entirely of roots, it's high time to pot on.

For container-grown plants, the rule is that younger plants should be potted on every one or two years, older ones about every four to five years. Spring (the start of the new growing season) is a good time to transfer houseplants. Never pot on while the plants are resting in winter, or while they're flowering. Always move plants into the next biggest size of container. To ensure proper drainage, put a potsherd (a broken fragment of clay pot) over the drainage hole. Over the next few weeks water moderately, but don't apply fertiliser and do make sure the plants are in a semi-shaded position.

Planting

When you're planting out container-grown seedlings take care not to bend or damage the roots: put them in the ground carefully. Shorten or trim any roots that are too long. It isn't difficult to put in plants that have root balls; if they've been grown in peat or paper pots and the roots are already starting to show through the sides, rapid growth is guaranteed.

Contact with the soil is important, so once you've put the seedlings into the holes you've made for them, firm them in well. Then water them, so that any spaces within the root system get filled with moist earth.

When the seedlings are large enough to handle, prick them out.

With peat pots, the shell is an integral part of the root ball.

Containers for raising and growing on plants

Plastic trays are lightweight, easy to disinfect and easy to clean. Wooden trays become heavy once they're saturated with moisture and provide a good breeding ground for fungal diseases.

Smaller amounts of seed can be accommodated in **pots and pans**. I'd also strongly recommend the use of **propagation trays**. These consist of a lower section with a built-in heating element (an electric heating cable) and a plastic cover. The localised heat means they can also be used to raise plants inside the greenhouse very economically.

Clay pots have porous sides. This helps to aerate the roots, as long as the permeability is not reduced by dirt and nutrient deposits. **Plastic pots** pose no such problems. They're impermeable, so there's no evaporation through the sides of the pot. The smooth walls are inhospitable to pathogens, and their low weight is another advantage. However, because they're difficult to dispose of, and place a burden on refuse systems, they're being replaced with **recyclable pots** made from paper, timber waste and other reusable materials. The same strictures apply to **plastic lattice pots**. They're put in the ground along with the plants; later, after the harvest or after flowering, they should be taken out of the ground so they don't turn up again on the compost heap or the beds.

Peat pots, made from a mixture of nutrient-enriched peats, are ideal, though environmentally-minded gardeners may prefer degradable pots. These pots give the young plants a very good start; after planting out, the roots grow through the peat shell, which has been incorporated into the root ball. **Peat pellets** are thick tablets that swell up into little peat pots after a few minutes in water. A plastic net holds the medium together; the roots can grow through it easily.

Choosing vegetables to grow

Cool house

If the greenhouse is run as a cool house and heated to temperatures of up to 50–54°F (10–12°C) to keep it frost-free, frost-sensitive plants can overwinter in it, e.g. container-grown plants, fuchsias and pelargoniums. It can also be used for propagation and for growing on seedlings that have been planted out. Give them additional protection by covering them with fleece in very cold weather.

To start the season in February or March you can plant kohl rabi, cabbage and lettuce seedlings. You can buy in seedlings of certain types from a garden centre or nursery. For the earliest sowings, consider radish, carrots, cress and loose-leaf (cut-and-come-again) lettuce. Sow them at the same time as the first plantings. Space cabbage lettuce 8 × 10 in (20 × 25 cm) apart, with about 16 plants per sq yd (20 plants/m²). In weed-free borders you can sow radishes between the rows, but this involves more work (because of the cultivation procedures and ground preparation required) and must be done carefully. Lettuce seedlings should be planted out on level ground — important for the formation of the heads. Water them thoroughly and ventilate them well; ideally the plants should be reasonably dry by nightfall. For kohl rabi, use the same spacing or slightly greater, up to 10 × 10 in (25 × 25 cm) which gives about 13 plants per sq yd (16 plants/m²).

Kohl rabi can also be grown in conjunction with cabbage lettuce. Stump rooted carrots along with radish are a useful early crop to sow direct in greenhouse borders. Radish demands a well-drained soil. Wet soils with little aeration produce bad roots. Rather than sowing them at regular intervals in the drills, these should be **station-sown**: sow a few seeds *together* at appropriate intervals, and thin them out later.

Like cress and loose-leaf lettuce, radish is a quick-maturing crop. It should be grown in rows about 4 in (10 cm) apart, and 2.5 in (6 cm) apart within the rows, giving upwards of 130 plants per sq yd (160/m²). But spacing is not too critical as long as they aren't overcrowded.

You can sow culinary herbs such as parsley, dill and chervil at the beginning of the season. Overwintered parsley roots and clumps of chives lifted in from the garden can also be started into growth.

Once the early crops have finished, main crops can follow. These include tomatoes, cucumbers and sweet peppers. When the summer crops have been

gathered the greenhouse can be used for a range of activities, e.g. forcing chicory or rhubarb under a blacked-out bench (darkness is vital for both). The chicory is sown in spring, thinned out and lifted, trimmed, and brought into the greenhouse to produce blanched shoots. The rhubarb crowns (roots) are lifted out of the ground early in winter, trimmed and brought into the greenhouse after frosting to produce blanched stems.

Further items on the calendar for planting and sowing at the beginning of September are cabbage lettuce (early variety) and radish. These are possibly the best plants to try out and gain experience from. Corn salad and spinach can be sown in mid-September, and offer another good way to make full use of the cool greenhouse.

Temperate greenhouse

The temperature range 50-63/64°F (10-17/18°C) opens up further possibilities, with cultivation starting earlier than in the cool greenhouse. Since the greenhouse isn't simply frost-free, cabbage lettuce, kohl rabi and radish can be planted or sown in early February in areas with good light. As a result these crops are harvested sooner, leaving space for tomatoes, cucumbers, sweet peppers and melons from mid-April.

The cool greenhouse provides plenty of scope for growing vegetables intensively.

Plants are grown in a similar way to the cool house, though the heating gives cultivation advantages in spring, autumn and winter. There's scope to get busy as early as January.

In January, some of the rhubarb root stocks that were lifted in autumn or winter can be planted in the greenhouse border (while others are forced in darkness). You can start pulling after five weeks.

Further early jobs include sowing seed for summer flowers that need to be raised in seed trays, and starting overwintered dahlia root stocks and begonia tubers into growth. There are also pelargoniums, fuchsias and other plants for the balcony and patio, and container-grown plants to start off, as well as early potatoes to sprout etc.

Cultivating plants isn't always easy for the relative beginner, but it's always worth having a go to get the experience.

The table overleaf brings together commonly grown varieties of vegetable for outdoor beds which can be raised in the greenhouse, and shows the most important dates. Seed quantities have been calculated so that you can select the best plants.

During the day, the boundary between cool and temperate greenhouse is fluid. If the sun is shining, then the cool house moves higher up the scale of warmth, at least in the day.

Vegetables for outdoor cultivation, seedlings raised in a small greenhouse

vegetable	seeds per gram	germination in days	sowing month	planting-out month	plant spacing in inches (cm)	for a 10m² plot: nos. of plants	seeds (g)
cabbage lettuce	800-1200	6-10	begMar.	beg. Apr.	8×10 (20×25)	200	0.4
cauliflower, early	130-200	6-8	beg. Feb.	mid-Apr.	20×20 (50×50)	40	0.4
cauliflower, summer	280-370	6-8	end-Mar.	end-May	20×20 (50×50)	40	0.4
celeriac & celery	2000-2900	14-20	end-Feb.	mid-May	20×12 (50×30)	66	0.1
cucumbers	35-45	4-4	mid-Apr.	mid-May	48×10 (120×25)	33	1.0
dwarf beans (in peat pots)	1.5-4.0	5-9	end-Apr.	mid-May	16×16 (40×40)	62*	200
kohl rabi	120-130	5-8	mid-Feb.	beg.Apr.	10×10 (25×25)	160	1.0
melons	30-35	6-8	beg.Apr.	mid-May	24×32 (60×80)	21	1.0
Peppers, red & green	170-220	12-15	mid-Mar.	end-May	16×20 (40×50)	62	1.0
red cabbage, early	270-330	6-8	beg.Feb.	mid Apr.	20×20 (50×50)	40	0.3
runner beans (in peat pots)	1.5-4.0	5-9	end-Apr.	mid-May	24×24 (60×60)	28*	100
savoy cabbage, early	300-380	6-8	beg.Feb.	mid-Apr.	20×20 (50×50)	40	0.3
tomatoes	300-370	8-14	beg.Mar.	mid-May	16×20 (40×50)	55	0.3
white cabbage, early	270-320	6-8	beg.Feb.	mid-Apr.	20×20 (50×50)	40	0.3

*sown in groups.

Note: Seed counts and germination times may vary considerably. Precise sowing times depend on conditions in your region, and on light levels in your greenhouse.

Overwintering tub plants and the first seedlings.

The warm greenhouse

If cost is not a problem, the warm greenhouse can be heated to temperatures as high as 64–75°F (18–24°C). The powerful heating system can provide ideal conditions even for plants needing a lot of warmth. It's also valuable as a place for propagating plants.

Experienced greenhouse gardeners can find jobs to do here throughout the year. Enthusiasts of the less common plants can tend their collections of exotic rarities; it's more the realm of the gardener who likes to be surrounded by orchids or bromeliads from the tropics.

The summary chart shows suggestions for vegetables that can be grown in heated greenhouses. For greenhouses without heating, the cultivation plan should be shifted more towards the late spring.

Making full use of a small heatable greenhouse, with eight main types of vegetable (timings may vary from one district to another)

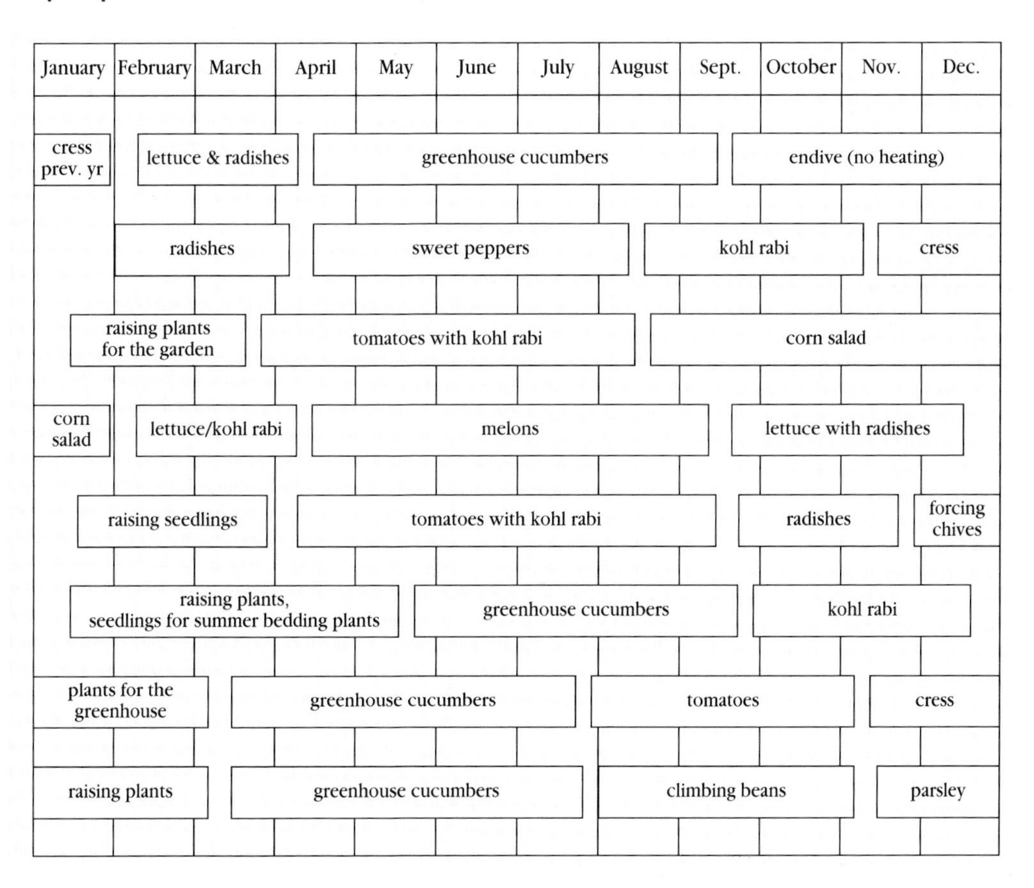

Applying fertilisers

A planting scheme is an essential part of this, so that the crop rotation is properly observed. Soil care is the basis of healthy plant growth, and you also need to think about supplying nutrients in an environmentally sensitive way.

You can introduce significant quantities of nutrients with organic materials like horse manure, garden compost, mulches and the residues of previous crops; remember this when you're working out how much fertiliser to apply. It might also be a good idea to have a soil sample tested. Keep your sowing and planting well spaced out, give water only when and where it's needed and provide plenty of ventilation. All these things help to keep pests and diseases at bay. Fertiliser requirements are given on page 50.

Greenhouse and cold frame, looking almost professional.

Vegetables for beginners

Chinese cabbage

Have a go with Chinese cabbage. Be warned, though: they're prone to running to seed or bolting when days are short. The seed is sown in batches (successional sowing) from the beginning of January to the end of February, with seedlings planted out from the beginning of February till the beginning of April. The cabbage is ready to cut from March until about

mid-May in good light areas. You'll need 'temperate' conditions of 57-61°F (14-16°C) to raise the seedlings, but once they're planted out they'll tolerate temperatures of 54-57°F (12-14°C) in the day and as low as 37°F (3°C) at night. Don't let them dry out, or they may bolt As Chinese cabbage can't tolerate high humidity, ventilate it in good time. The recommended spacing between plants is 12 × 14 in (30 × 35 cm). With 7-8 mature plants per square metre, you should achieve yields of about 5 kg/m².

Corn salad

Corn salad, also known as Lamb's lettuce, is tasty and full of vitamins and minerals, making it an ideal winter vegetable for the cool area. It's suitable for growing as a follow-on crop in areas that are kept from 41 to 54°F (5-12°C); sow it between August and October. In an unheated greenhouse it can take up to three or four months to mature, depending on the weather conditions and when it was sown. The growing time is shorter in a temperate greenhouse. Corn salad should be sown in rows at a depth of 1-2 cm and 4 in (10 cm) apart: this requires 2-2.5 g/m² of seed. If the plants are grown too close together, you risk mildew attack.

Don't let the plants dry out during the first 4-6 weeks, and provide plenty of ventilation. On no account apply fertiliser 'just in case'. The ground usually contains enough nutrients from the preceding crop, and there is often too much nitrogen.

Left *Chinese cabbage is becoming increasingly popular, but is not yet very widely grown.*

Right *Kohl rabi can be grown almost all year round.*

Kohl rabi

This can be grown virtually all year round. If the seed is sown at the beginning of January, the seedlings can be planted out in mid-March and the crop harvested late April or early May. With successional sowings at fortnightly intervals, kohl rabi can be available into June. For autumn planting, sow outdoors from early to late August and plant out from early to late September. The crop should be ready from the beginning of November to the middle of December. The experimentally

Left *Some varieties of radish can be amazingly tender.*
Right *Spinach is a sensible way of using space in the cool greenhouse.*

minded gardener can sow at the beginning of November, plant in mid-January and have the vegetable on the table in March.

The plants should be spaced at 10 × 10 in (25 × 25 cm) intervals, giving 13 plants per square yard (16 plants/m²). Don't plant them too deep; there's a risk of rot if the base of the globe is allowed to rest on the ground. Spring plants like to be kept at 59°F (15°C) by day and 50°F (10°C) by night; autumn plantings need 50°F (10°C) and 43°F (6°C). Give them ventilation once the temperature reaches a maximum of 68°F (20°C). Growing out of season can be tricky.

Kohl rabi are moderate feeders, and like a pH of 6-7.

Radishes

Radishes are one of the quick-maturing vegetables; depending on when they were planted and the time of year, they are soon ready to pull. To grow well in winter they need a good light. For the best results avoid sowing them too thickly, or the plants fail to develop good roots. Rather than sowing broadcast, sow them in half-inch (1-cm) deep drills which are 3-4 in (8-10 cm) apart; thin the seedlings to 2.5 in (6 cm) apart. To produce about 150 plants/m² you'll need at least 2 g of seed.

A temperature of 54-59°F (12-15°C) is desirable for germination, but later on daytime temperatures of 50-54°F (10-12°C) and 43-46°F (6-8°C) at night will be adequate, depending on the time of year. If you pay careful attention to ventilation, heating, watering and spacing you should avoid the risk of fungal disease.

Radishes are very suitable for combining with cabbage lettuce; sow the radish seed a little while before the lettuce is planted out, sowing in drills between the rows where the lettuce will be. Choose a variety that's suitable for the time of year. It's also possible to start the seedlings in seed trays and plant them out later. Popular varieties include 'Black Spanish', 'Cherry Belle', 'Helro' and 'Rota'.

The longer forms of radishes are mainly grown outdoors, but can be cultivated under glass. They come in various colours from black to white, via brown, violet, red and pink. You must prepare the ground thoroughly and ensure it's well aerated. They are best sown directly into their final positions. Another possibility is to start the seedlings in peat pots, sowing two seeds in each pot and taking one of the seedlings out later. Long radishes should be planted out 8 × 8 in (20 × 20 cm) or 8 × 7 in (20 × 18 cm) apart; smaller ones are sown 5 × 6 in (12 × 15 cm) apart, not continuously but station-sown, putting in two seeds at each station and thinning to one later. Popular varieties include 'Long White Icicle' and 'China Rose'.

The temperature required is 50-57°F (10-14°C) by day and 41-47°F (5-7°C) at night. Don't allow the plants to dry out, but keep humidity levels low, with good ventilation. These are important factors in ensuring successful growth.

Spinach

In a good light area it makes sense to use the cool greenhouse for spinach rather than leaving it empty. Sow in November/December and harvest in March/April, or rather earlier if there's a bit of heat. The seeds should be sown in drills about 1 in (2-3 cm) deep and 5-6 in (12-15 cm) apart. There is a danger of mildew if the plants are too close together. Over a period the yield should be around 2 kg/m^2. The greenhouse must have good ventilation and the temperature should be kept at 50-59°F (10-15°C). Water adequately, but not frequently, and see that the plants have dried off before the evening. Popular varieties are 'Medania', 'Triton' (F1 hybrid) and 'Sigma Leaf'.

Endive

This is another vegetable worth trying, as a substitute for lettuce in autumn, winter and spring. Endives take about seven weeks to reach maturity for a spring crop, sowing at the end of December. If the seed's sown outdoors in July, they should be ready for harvesting from November. Plant them out at a distance of 10 × 10 in (25 × 25 cm); provide water and ventilation as for cabbage lettuce. Water early enough for the plants to dry off before nightfall — this avoids any danger of rot. Temperatures around 50°F (10°C) or even down as far as 41°F (5°C) are quite adequate. Blanching, done by covering the plant with a pot and blocking the drainage hole to exclude light, makes the leaves more succulent.

You can sow endives straight into their final position in drills 0.6 in (1.5 cm) deep and 12 in (30 cm) apart; for outdoor culture thin to 12-14 in (30-35 cm), though transplanting is more convenient. Recommended varieties are 'Moss Curled', 'Batavian Green', 'Eminence', 'Markamt' and 'Ione'.

Spring onions

These can be grown as a catch crop. Ideally you should sow them directly into the greenhouse border in February/March or in August, but they can be sown at any other time if there's space for them. The seed has a long germination time of 14-25 days. Do not sow broadcast, but thinly in drills along the edge next to other vegetables.

Start with vegetables that are easier to grow. Draw up a planting scheme and work out the growing space needed for each vegetable and the amounts of fertiliser needed. This ensures that the crops are rotated when further crops are planted.

The end of the season is in sight: the tomatoes are still ripening but the garden onions are already drying.

Vegetables for enthusiasts

Cabbage lettuce

A November sowing, with planting out in January and harvesting at the end of March, needs about 100 days, but you can cut this timetable in half by starting the process in March. If you do, plant the seedlings out in April and they'll be ready to cut in May. Lettuces need plenty of light; that's why it isn't all that easy to grow them in autumn and winter. Don't try to grow winter lettuce in a poor light area. On the other hand, their temperature requirements are modest; in spring they'll tolerate daytime temperatures of 54-59°F (12-15°C) and night-time ones of 43-46°F (6-8°C). Ventilate above 64°F (18°C). Plant them out at a distance of 8 × 10 in (20 × 25 cm), and don't plant them too deep because of the danger of rot. When choosing a variety, think about its suitability for the growing season you've chosen.

I recommend loose-leaf (cut-and-come-again) lettuce as an alternative salad crop for the winter. It should be planted in rows 6 in (15 cm) apart.

The sweet pepper needs greenhouse conditions similar to those required by tomatoes.

Sweet peppers

The pepper's temperature needs are broadly similar to those of the tomato: 68°F (20°C) by day and around 61°F (16°C) at night. The plants should be kept as dry as possible, as condensation can produce rot in flowers and fruits. Generally, starting to sow in late February for planting in late April or early May is an acceptable timetable. The seedlings are pricked out into trays 2 × 2 in (5 × 5 cm) apart, or preferably put straight into 3.5-in (9-cm) pots. Plant them out 16 × 20 in (40 × 50 cm) apart. It takes about ten weeks to get from sowing to planting out, but it's only about 6-8 weeks from planting out to harvest. Keep the plants well watered during this growth period and watch out for pests. This is a case where soil or localised heating will prove its worth, because soil tempera tures below 50°F (10°C) inhibit growth. Support tall-growing varieties. Generally three to five stems are allowed to form, and a length of string is put around them to stop them sprouting.

French beans

It's worth having a go with these, although they can be quite tricky to grow. Start by putting three beans each in 3.5-in (9-cm) pots. Germination takes about two weeks and requires a temperature of 68°F (20°C), but beans need 59-64°F (15-18°C) while they're growing. Ventilate regularly.

The soil should be light and rich in humus, but it isn't usually necessary to apply nitrogen. Space the plants 20 × 16 in (50 × 40 cm) apart. Train the shoots of climbing French beans onto strings or wires to support them, and stop the dwarf beans from flopping by supporting them with canes and string. Pinching out the main tip promotes the formation of side shoots and the start of flowering. It also helps to increase the yield. With climbing French beans, don't start copious watering until the flowers have formed; this helps to keep the young pods on the plant.

Water the plants from below, without spraying the leaves; you could use a trickle system (see page 28). April plantings produce a crop of about 10 lb/sq yd (4 kg/m²) from June to the end of July. By planting later you can extend the bean harvest right into the autumn. Dwarf beans have smaller yields of up to 3 lb/sq yd (1.5 kg/m²).

Climbing beans in the greenhouse.

Sweet melons

If you sow the seed in mid-January, you can plant out the seedlings in mid-March and harvest the melons at the end of May; but don't try this unless the light in your area is excellent. You can shorten the total cultivation time by sowing later, at the beginning of April; the fruits are ready from July onwards. Sow directly into pots. Germination requires temperatures of at least 68°F (20°C) and preferably 77-86°F (25-30°C); a heated propagating bed is useful. Plant out 32 in (80 cm) apart in all directions in well-prepared soil. The soil temperature needs to be 59-64°F (15-18°C), with daytime temperatures of 77°F (25°C) and 54-59°F (12-15°C) at night. A localised heating system will help here.

If you start cultivation early you can't rely on bees for pollination, so use a fine paint brush to transfer the pollen from the male flowers to the female stigma. Pinch out the growing point above the fifth leaf; stop side-shoots after the sixth leaf.

Favourite vegetables

Aubergines (egg-plants)

These require even warmth. Sow them between the end of February and April, and transfer them to small pots later. Once they've got going they need a temperature of around 61-64°F (16-18°C) in a temperate or warm greenhouse. From the middle of May, plant them out into the cool greenhouse 20 × 20 in (50 × 50 cm) apart.

It's a good idea to tie the plants to stakes, or to train two shoots up on strings. Stop the main shoot(s) after the sixth leaf, and remove superfluous side-shoots every fortnight. The fruit is ready to cut from mid-August. Water from below and ventilate well.

Aubergines require similar conditions to tomatoes, but need a higher temperature.

Cucumbers

For early cultivation, it's best to get plants from your garden centre or nursery. Especially at the early stages, cucumbers have special requirements for warmth and humidity. The temperature can be up to 77°F (25°C) during the day and 64-68°F (18-20°C) at night, and humidity should be around 80-90 per cent. Cucumbers should be spaced at 16-20 in (40-50 cm) intervals, with 40 in (1 m) between rows. The earth should be loose-structured, fertile and rich in humus; many gardeners use very well-rotted horse manure. Cucumbers can also be grown on straw bales.

It's best to plant cucumbers on mounds and pile up more earth or compost every so often when roots appear on the surface. The ground temperature should be 60°F (15°C); growth will be improved if you mulch with horse manure or use localised heating.

Some days after planting, fasten strings above the plants at one end and tie the other ends to the greenhouse frame. Stop the main shoot of each plant when it reaches the roof. Nip out the side-shoots again beyond the first leaf and the first developing fruit. Humidity is important, and for large-scale growing an electronic humidifier is useful, but spraying water on paths and on the ground will also do the trick. Use a hygrometer to check the humidity. Don't give cucumbers a lot of ventilation; in fact they should have none at all for a few days after they've been planted out. Cucumbers need a lot of water, so a trickle system helps. It's difficult to grow cucumbers late in the year, in autumn and winter, and, aside from any other problems, you could run up large heating bills.

When choosing cucumbers look for resistance to mildew, scab, leaf spot, gummosis and mosaic virus.

Tomatoes

These are sown in pans, pots or trays from January to April, depending on the planting scheme, and are ready for planting out between March and June. They're ready for picking between June and December. Germination takes two weeks at a temperature of 68°F (20°C). Cooler temperatures prolong the germination time. A crop of up to 25 lb/sq yd (10 kg/m^2) can be expected. Plant out at 16 × 16-20 in (40 × 40-50 cm). Using grow-bags will ensure they get a clean start, free from disease. Each grow-bag contains potting compost and will accommodate three plants. Tomatoes do best with plenty of ventilation and low humidity; don't spray the plants with water. They like a sunny situation, not shade. Water regularly and feed with a liquid complete fertiliser (organic or mineral-based).

Fruit formation depends a lot on temperature; flowers won't set too well below 54°F (12°C). The range 68-82°F (20-28°C) is good for the development of the pollen grains, which degenerate above 85°F (30°C). It doesn't matter at all if the overnight temperature sometimes drops to 60°F (15°C) or less.

Tie tomato plants to supporting canes, or train them around strings, and keep removing side shoots. Take care that the plants don't dry out; ideally use a drip-watering system, as otherwise the flowers may drop, and there can be problems with blossom-end rot (especially if the plants are in grow-bags). To get the fruits to set, shake the inflorescences three times a week (twice in sunny weather). This promotes pollination. Also make sure the temperature is right, there's plenty of air, and the relative humidity is between 60 and 70 per cent. If it is below 50 per cent, the pollen tubes may dry out before fertilisation; in poor conditions, 'setting' spray may assist setting. If humidity is above 80 per cent, the pollen grains stick together.

Tomatoes head the list of greenhouse gardeners' favourites.

Herbs

Most culinary herbs are annuals, and like the perennial ones they're familiar from the garden. Your greenhouse gives you the chance to provide fresh herbs even during the cold season.

Cress

Because it develops so quickly, cress can be sown and used at two-weekly intervals from autumn to spring. It's usual to sow it in trays and pans, but it can be sown in the greenhouse border, in rows 3-4 in (8-10 cm) apart. Cress is always sown thickly. It's also a good idea to cover the seed with a 0.1-in (3-mm) deep layer of sand; this keeps the brown seed cases out of the way.

Dill

Dill is sown in the border in early spring (in the greenhouse) or later (out of doors). Sow it in rows 6 in (15 cm) apart, or better still in a single row, perhaps as an edging plant. Successional sowing is best, so that fresh dill is always available at the time of year when vitamins are in short supply. Its temperature requirements, at 59°F (15°C) by day and 50°F (10°C) by night, match conditions in the temperate greenhouse. Like most other herbs, dill needs virtually no fertilisers.

Chives

These hardy perennials are sown in the greenhouse in spring. To raise enough plants for 10 sq ft (1 m^2) spaced at 8 x 6 in (20 x 15 cm) intervals, you need a small packet of seed. Plant out in clumps with 15-20 individual plants to a clump. In the following year dig up the root balls and heel them in to a greenhouse border for 'forcing'; however, they must first have been thoroughly frosted.

Parsley

This is another garden plant, but it's also very suitable for starting off indoors. Sow in small pots in February/March in the temperate greenhouse at 46-50°F (8-10°C); the plants can then be planted out into the garden in clumps. Another approach is to raise seedlings all year round, so the fresh green leaves are always available. Like chives, parsley roots can be heeled in to greenhouse borders, or more conveniently grown in pots and brought in for protection in the winter, to ensure continuity.

There's plenty of scope for experimenting with other herbs. Try protecting other hardy herbs, or sowing annual ones out of season.

Chives must be well frosted before they are brought indoors and put under the benching to be forced.

Making full use of the space under the benching

The space under the benching or in the greenhouse borders should be used sensibly.

Parsley roots can be lifted from garden beds and put in the earth at such a depth that only the tops show. And if roots are put in 5-6 in (12-14 cm) pots, even at 50°F (10°C), they'll provide enough fresh parsley for a family of four all winter.

Chives provide a tasty, mineral-rich garnish for the kitchen at a time of year when vitamins are in short supply. Choose strongly-developed root balls, dig them up in winter, leave them to get well frosted and then bring them one by one into the greenhouse. Watering them with warm water at 104°F (40°C) on several occasions helps them to start growing.

Onion greens can keep the family supplied all winter. For 100 onions 2-2.5 lb (1-1.2 kg) of sets, 1-1.5 in (2.5-3.5) cm in diameter, will be needed; they'll be available as a by-product of the main onion crop. Planted successionally at a distance of 2 × 3 in (5 × 8 cm), they will produce a continuous supply of fresh onion greens.

Chicory yields some tasty blanched shoots if forced in darkness in a warm greenhouse. It can also be grown by planting deeply in a greenhouse border. Start forcing at the beginning of December, and continue it successionally to give a longer cropping period. Dig out the earth to a depth of 8 in (20 cm) and plant the roots in rows 2 in (5 cm) apart. After watering, cover them to a depth of 10 in (25 cm) with a light, loamy growing medium. With a soil temperature of 50-59°F (10-15°C), harvesting can begin 3-4 weeks later. The shoots, or chicons, are up to 10 in (25 cm) long; harvest them by carefully laying the individual rows bare.

Chicory roots are obtained by cultivation in the open ground, growing from seed sown at 8-10 g seed/10 m². The rows should be 10-12 in (25-30 cm) apart, and the plants are thinned to 4-6 in (10-15 cm) apart within the rows. To plant 10 sq ft (1 m²) of ground with roots for forcing requires 36 sq yd (30 m²) of open ground.

Rhubarb. Three-year-old plants are used, and the clumps are exposed to the frost before they are forced. You'll need eight rhubarb plants for an area of 1 sq yd (1 m²). Keep them evenly moist. You can start pulling the rhubarb stems 4-6 weeks after the clumps have been brought indoors. After forcing, plant the clumps in the garden; they can be used for forcing again after three years.

Mushrooms. As well as the usual white cultivated mushroom, oyster mushrooms are suitable candidates for the space under the benching or in a dark shed. Mushroom growing has changed a lot in recent years, with specialist firms selling complete growing kits with full instructions.

Raising, requirements and treatment

The time needed to raise these plants varies from one genus to another. The process begins with sowing and germination, goes on to pricking out or potting up in containers, and culminates when the young plants are planted out. Sow the seed in trays, pots or pans filled with seed compost. It's best to prick out straight into small pots, so the plants can form individual root balls. This means that nothing can check their progress when they're planted out, and they can grown on undisturbed. You'll need green fingers and great sensitivity to judge sowing times, temperature requirements and further treatment.

The greenhouse gardener's pride and joy: busy lizzie (Impatiens) raised from seed in the greenhouse.

Summer flowers

There are annual and biennial genera. Annuals are plants whose entire life cycle is usually confined to a single growing year. Some need to be raised from seed in protected conditions before they are planted out; others are sown directly in the garden, but you can also raise them in the greenhouse so they will flower earlier.

Biennial (two-year) summer flowers overwinter after they've been raised from seed and bloom in their second year. They include wallflowers, forget-me-nots and daisies.

How to raise well-known annuals as bedding-out plants

(Some genera such as *Clarkia, Godetia, Nigella, Phacelia, Tropaeolum* etc. can also be sown directly in the open ground without raising the seedlings indoors)

name botanical	common	sowing Feb.	Mar.	Apr.	seeds per gram (approx.)	germi nation in days
Ageratum	floss flower	×	×	-	5,000	8-10
Alcea	hollyhock	-	×	×	100	10
Amaranthus	love-lies-bleeding	-	×	×	1,500	15
Antirrhinum	snapdragon	×	×	-	6,000	15-20
Arctotis	African daisy	-	-	×	400	15-20
Artemisia	wormwood	-	×	×	30,000	10
Asarina	asarina	×	-	-	2,000	10-14
Begonia	begonia	×	-	-	80,000	12
Brachycome	Swan River daisy	-	×	-	6,000	15-20
Browallia	bush violet	-	×	-	350	15
Celosia	cockscomb	-	×	-	1,200	10
Clarkia	clarkia	-	×	-	3,000	12
Cleome	spider flower	-	×	-	4,000	15
Cobaea	cup-and-saucer vine	-	×	-	15	12 cl.
Coreopsis	tickseed	-	×	-	3,500	15
Cosmea	osmea	-	×	×	250	12
Dolichos	hyacinth bean	-	×	-	5-10	12 cl.
Gaillardia	blanket flower	-	×	-	400	15
Gazania	treasure flower	-	×	-	200	10-15
Godetia	godetia	-	×	-	3,500	15
Helichrysum	everlasting flower	-	×	×	1,300	10-14
Impatiens	busy lizzie	-		×	120	10
Ipomoea	morning glory	-	×	×	50	15 cl.
Kochia	summer cypress	-	×	×	1,200	15
Lathyrus	sweet pea	-	×	×	12	15-20 cl.
Lobelia	lobelia	×	×	-	30,000	15-20
Malope	malope	-	×	×	300	14
Matthiola	stock	-	×	×	700	15
Mimulus	monkey flower	-	×	×	30,000	14
Mirabilis	four o'clock flower	-	×	×	10	10-15
Nigella	love-in-a-mist	-	×	×	500	10-14
Petunia	petunia	×	×	-	6,000	10-14
Phacelia	phacelia	-	×	-	600	14-20
Phlox drummondii	annual phlox	-	×	-	400	10-18
Portulaca	sun plant	-	×	-	10,000	15
Salpiglossis	salpiglossis	-	×	-	4,500	12-15
Salvia	salvia	-	×	-	400	10-15
Sanvitalia	creeping zinnia	-	×	-	1,200	15
Scabiosa	scabious	-	×	-	300	12-20
Schizanthus	butterfly flower	×	×	-	1,500	15
Tagetes	marigold	-	×	×	300	10
Thunbergia alata	black-eyed Susan	×	-	-	50	10-14 cl.
Tropaeolum	nasturtium	-	×	×	8-20	12-16 cl.
Verbena	verbena	×	×	-	300	15-21
Zinnia	youth and old age	-	×	×	150-400	4-6

cl.= climber

Herbaceous perennials

These hardy flowering and foliage plants live for a number of years. Their non-woody shoots die down to the root stock annually, and grow afresh from buds in or just above the earth each year. Herbaceous perennials overwinter by such means as rhizomes, root stocks, rosettes, and runners. Many can be propagated by various vegetative methods.

Herbaceous perennial lovers with greenhouses raise their own plants from seed for convenience, though many can be raised out of doors. The rarer genera and species may be easier to obtain as seeds, and can be grown in larger numbers.

Herbaceous perennials are sown in pans, small trays or pots, though outdoors they can be sown in shallow drills. Cover the seeds with a little sand and don't let them dry out.

The genera marked with an asterisk (*) in the table opposite ideally require special treatment before sowing: **vernalisation** (exposure to the cold). Most are alpines: in their natural habitat the seeds fall in autumn, onto ground that hasn't yet frozen, and overwinter under the snow. Changing temperatures between 32°F (0°C) and 40°F (5°C) provide the stimulus needed for germination.

This means it's best to presoak the seed, sow it in seed trays or pots, keep it at 50-60°F (10-15°C) for 2-3 weeks — and then, ideally, cover it with snow. This may be possible, because most of these seeds are sown between November and February; if there's no snow, you could try plunging the pots in an open sand bed outside, or putting the seed in a refrigerator for a short period before sowing in spring. *Adonis vernalis* and most primulas are an exception. If their seed is sown as soon as it's been gathered, it germinates without difficulty; otherwise they should be treated like the others, which need pre-chilling.

*Bleeding heart (*Dicentra*) can be raised from seed, too.*

Herbaceous perennials

botanical name	common name	sowing month(s)	recommended germination temperature in °F (°C)	average germination time in days
Achillea	yarrow	Feb.-Apr.	64 (18)	15-20
Aconitum	monkshood	Jan.-Mar.	57 (14) *	5-50
Adonis vernalis	adonis vernalis	May-Aug.	59 (15) *	30-50
Alyssum	alyssum	Mar.-May	64 (18)	14-21
Anemone pulsatilla	pasque flower	Oct.-Mar.	61 (16) *	35-50
Aquilegia caerulea	columbine	Jan.-May	64 (18)	20-35
Arabis caucasica	arabis caucasica	Jan.-June	59 (15)	20-30
Armeria maritima	sea pink	Jan.-June	59 (15)	20-30
Aster	michaelmas daisy	Dec.-June	59-64 (15-18)	14-20
Bergenia	large-leaved saxifrage	Dec.-June	64 (18)	20-30
Campanula	bellflower	Dec.-Apr.	64 (18)	15-30
Centaurea	cornflower	Jan.-June	64 (18)	10-14
Cerastium	snow-in-summer	Dec.-July	64 (18)	14-30
Chrysanthemum maximum	shasta daisy	Jan.-May	64 (18)	12-20
Coreopsis grandiflora	tickseed	Jan.-June	64 (18)	15-21
Delphinium	delphinium	Dec.-June	59 (15)	20-30
Dianthus plumarius	pink	Mar.-July	59 (15)	7-14
Dicentra	bleeding heart	Aug.-Oct./ Jan.-Mar.	64 (18) *	15-20
Digitalis	foxglove	Mar.-June	64 (18)	15-20
Dodecatheon	shooting stars	Oct.-Mar.	64 (18) *	20-40
Doronicum	leopard's bane	Feb.-May	59 (15)	15-21
Erigeron	fleabane	Feb.-Apr.	59 (15)	20-30
Gaillardia aristata	blanket flower	Apr.-July	64 (18)	14-20
Gentiana	gentian	Dec.-Mar.	64 (18) *	25-40
Geum	avens	Feb.-May	64 (18)	20-30
Gypsophila	baby's breath	Mar.-July	61 (16)	14-20
Helenium	sneezeweed	Jan.-June	61 (16)	14-20
Heuchera	coral flower	Dec.-Apr.	64 (18)	10-20
Iberis sempervirens	candytuft	Jan.-May	59 (15)	14-20
Kniphofia	red hot poker	Jan.-May	64 (18)	14-20
Lathyrus latifolius	everlasting pea	Jan.-May	59 (15)	15-25
Lavandula	lavender	Dec.-Mar.	68 (20)	14-20
Liatris spicata	gay feathers	Jan.-June	64 (18)	20-30
Lupinus polyphyllus	perennial lupin	Dec.-June	61 (16)	14-20
Lychnis	campion	Jan.-May	64 (18)	14-25
Phlox paniculata	phlox paniculata	Dec.-Mar.	64 (18)	20-35
Physostegia virginiana	obedient plant	Jan.-May	61 (16)	20-25
Primula	primula	Feb.-May	59 (15)	18-30
Rudbeckia	coneflower	Jan.-June	64 (18)	15-20
Salvia	salvia	Jan.-May	68 (20)	14-20
Sedum	sedum	Feb.-May	59 (15)	14-20
Trollius	globeflower	Dec.-Mar.	59 (15) *	20-30
Veronica	speedwell	Feb.-May	64 (18)	14-20
Viola cornuta	horned violet	Feb.-Aug.	64 (18)	15-25

When calculating seed requirements, fractions of a gram are often sufficient, as with some genera 0.5 g of seed yields 1,000 plants. Plants marked with an asterisk (*) should ideally be exposed to the cold before sowing. Seed may not always be readily available.

Bedding and balcony plants

Plants for beds and borders, and for window boxes, bowls and tubs, are treated as annuals and are usually raised afresh each year. Some (geraniums, for instance) are often overwintered and then woken to new life the following year. It works, but the plant will start to become less attractive as early as the second year. It's far better to get young plants from cuttings taken in August so they can produce roots before the winter.

Fuchsias are the easiest plants to get through the winter, and this is always done with plants that have been trained as standards. But here, too, propagation by cuttings is successful, just as it is with verbenas and lantanas.

Other bedding and balcony plants (in other words the majority of genera and species used in this way) are propagated from seed.

The number of plants you'll need depends, of course, on the amount of space available for planting, but another factor is the orientation of the site. It wouldn't be very helpful to raise dozens of fuchsias and tuberous begonias if their final home is going to be in full sun. Both of them thrive in partial or even full shade. On the other hand, geraniums, verbenas, lantanas and salvias are among

A selection of common plants for flowerbed and balcony

botanical name	common name	propagation method	time	germination in days
Ageratum houstonianum	floss flower	seed	Feb.-Mar.	8-10
Alyssum maritimum syn. Lobularia maritima	sweet alyssum	seed	Feb.-Apr.	8-14
Begonia semperflorens	fibrous-rooted dwarf begonia	seed	Dec.-Feb.	20-22
Begonia tuberhybrida	tuberous hybrid begonia	seed/tubers	Dec.-Feb.	22-24 seed
Calceolaria integrifolia	slipper plant	seed	Dec.-Feb.	15-20
Celosia argentea	cockscomb	seed	Feb.-Apr.	7-14
Chrysanthemum frutescens & C.multicaule, paludosum	marguerite, autumn-flowering chrysanthemum	seed	Jan.-Mar.	10-14
Exacum affine	Arabian violet	seed	Dec.-May	14-20
Fuchsia	fuchsia	cutting	Jan.-Feb.	12 to root
Heliotropium arborescens	cherry pie	seed	Jan.-Mar.	14-20
Impatiens walleriana	busy lizzie	seed/cutting	Jan.-Apr.	10-18
Lantana Camara hybrids	lantana camara hybrids	cutting	Oct.-Nov.	-
Lobelia erinus	lobelia erinus	seed	Jan.-Mar.	7-14
Pelargonium zonale hybrids & *P. peltatum* hybrids	zonal & ivy-leaved geraniums	cutting/seed	Aug.-Sep./ Dec.-Jan	10-14 to root
Petunia	petunia	seed	Jan.-Mar.	10-14
Salvia splendens	salvia splendens	seed	Jan.-Mar.	10-15
Sanvitalia procumbens	creeping zinnia	seed	Mar.-Apr.	7-15
Tagetes erecta	African marigold	seed	Feb.-Apr.	7-14
Tagetes patula	French marigold	seed	Feb.-Apr.	7-14
Verbena hybrids	verbena hybrids	seed/cutting	Feb.-Apr./ Aug.-Sep.	20-30

the plants which can tolerate full sunlight.

Petunias, slipper plants (*Calceolaria*), busy lizzies (*Impatiens*) and *Begonia semperflorens* will tolerate warm conditions, but prefer to be protected from direct, hot sunlight at the early stages. Modern strains will thrive in most conditions.

Above Coreopsis *(tickseed), a genus that includes both herbaceous and annual species*

Below *Fuchsias are great favourites with greenhouse gardeners.*

recommended germination temperature in (°F (°C)	flowering time	height in inches (cm)	sunny (su) partial shade (ps)	
64-70 (18-21)	June-Oct.	6 (15)	su	
64-72 (18-22)	June-Oct.	4 (10)	su	ps
59-68 (15-20)	May-Oct.	4-6 (10-15)	su	ps
59-68 (15-20)	May-Oct.	6 (15)	su	ps
59 (15)	May-Oct.	8-16 (20-40)	su	ps
64 (18)	June-Oct.	8 (20)	su	
54-64 (12-18)	June-Oct.	10-12 (25-30)	su	ps
64 (18)	May-Oct.	6-8 (15-20)	su	ps
68 (20)	May-Oct.	depends on variety	ps	
64 (18)	May-Oct.	16 (40)	su	
68 (20)	May-Oct.	6/8/12 (15/20/30)	su	ps
50-54 (10-12)	Apr.-Oct.	12-20 (30-50)	su	ps
64 (18)	Apr.-Oct.	4/8/12 (10/20/30)	su	
59-64 (15-18)	May-Oct.	erect up to 12 (30), hanging shoots up to 40 in (100 cm)	su	
64-68 (18-20)	May-Oct.	8-12 (20-30)	su	ps
68 (20)	May-Oct.	10 (25)	su	
64 (18)	May-Oct.	8 (20)	su	ps
64 (18)	May-Oct.	24-36 (60-90)	su	ps
64 (18)	May-Oct.	8-12 (20-30)	su	ps
59-70 (15-21)	May-Oct.	6-18 (15-45)	su	

Container-grown plants for house and greenhouse

Some plants thrive only in warm situations. Others prefer moderate 'temperate' conditions. Others again like it decidedly cool. Many want cool surroundings only during the short days of winter, and require more heat from spring to autumn. Tropical plants are true to their original growth pattern when they are transplanted to temperate latitudes: they need higher temperatures and plenty of humidity.

These various demands differ not only between botanical families but also within genera. You need knowledge and sensitivity to cater for departures from the usual requirements.

There isn't space in this book for exhaustive information about the habits of all the common greenhouse plants. However, there are plenty of specialist books available which anyone with a particular interest in the field can go to for information, including some of the other books in this series.

On the next few pages you'll find summary tables that will give you at least some indication of temperature and other requirements. These tables list the important ornamental plants which can be grown in the greenhouse, with appropriate notes, but they can only give you a very general indication.

Some genera contain many species which differ in their demands for heat, humidity, light and ventilation, and also in the way their resting periods are handled.

Many plants have a cycle of growth phases and rest phases. In the wild, these phases are influenced by seasonal changes from moisture and warmth on the one hand to dryness and low temperatures on the other. Numerous greenhouse plants observe a period of rest in winter: during this period they should usually be kept cooler and drier.

If you want to surround yourself with plants that have differing requirements, it isn't easy to provide all the different temperatures that are needed if you've only got one space available. In

The classification of greenhouses according to the level to which they are heated should not be regarded as an inflexible set of rules. The traditional division is as follows (first/lower values for night-time, second/higher ones for daytime temperatures):
Warm house 63/64-75/79°F (17/18-24/26°C)
Temperate house 45/50-57/63°F (7/10-14/17°C)
Cool house with heating 41/45-50/54°F (5/7-10/12°C)
Overwintering house 32-41°F (0-5°C), i.e. frost-free.
It is no reflection on a gardener's skill if the thermometer in a 'temperate' greenhouse reads 72°F (22°C) at midday on warm days, despite open vents, or if it slips down to around 50°F (10°C) in the evening. After all, the daytime temperature depends on the sun.

this case the conditions must always be governed by the needs of the more valuable species. You'll simply have to accept that other plants won't be enjoying ideal conditions and won't, therefore, flourish as well as they might. If you can put up a dividing 'wall' up across your greenhouse, you'll be able to create two temperature zones, and to grow plants which have different needs.

These cool greenhouse plants have quite modest needs when

Cool greenhouse plants

Plants for the cool greenhouse which don't need much heat, i.e. 41-50°F (5-10°C) in winter and 59-64°F (15-18°C) in summer:

Abutilon striatum, spotted flowering maple
Agapanthus, African lily
Agave, agave
Albizia lophanta
Aloe, aloe
Araucaria, Norfolk Island pine
Aspidistra, aspidistra
Aucuba japonica, spotted laurel
Bougainvillea, bougainvillea
cacti
Callistemon, bottlebrush
Campanula, bellflower
Chlorophytum, spider plant
Citrus, lemon, orange
Coleus, coleus
Crassula, crassula
Cyperus papyrus, papyrus
Cytisus canariensis, broom
Datura, angels' trumpets
Dracaena draco, dragon tree
Erica gracilis, Cape heath
Echeveria, echeveria
Eugenia myrtifolia
Euonymus, spindle tree
Euphorbia milii, crown of thorns
Fatsia japonica, Japanese aralia
ferns:
  Polystichum, shield fern
  Pteris
Fuchsia, fuchsia
Gasteria, gasteria
Grevillea, silk oak
Hedera, ivy
Lachenalia, cape cowslip
Muehlenbeckia, muehlenbeckia
Myrtus, myrtle
Nerium, oleander
Oplismenus, basket grass
palms:
  Chamaerops humilis, dwarf fan palm
  Phoenix canariensis, Canary Island date palm
  Trachycarpus fortunei, windmill palm
Parthenocissus, Virginia creeper
Passiflora, passion flower
Pelargonium, geranium
Plumbago capensis, Cape leadwort
Primula malacoides, fairy primrose
Primula obconica
Punica granatum, pomegranate
Rochea, rochea
Schizanthus, butterfly flower
Senecio cruentus
Solanum, winter cherry
Sparmannia africana, African hemp
Stapelia, carrion flower
Yucca, palm lily

The greenhouse provides a home for many plants that have grown too large, alongside container-grown plants that are overwintering here.

it comes to watering: in winter water them little and carefully. Give them an airy situation in good light.

In summer, some of the undemanding plants can stand in containers in the garden and on the patio. At this time of year nearly all of them prefer a light and sunny situation, but mostly prefer to be protected from intense, direct sunlight. Of course, they need correspondingly more moisture. It's essential for the plants' welfare to give them more water and an occasional application of fertiliser, and to spray the leaves every so often.

Temperate area

Plants for the temperate greenhouse make greater demands than those for the cool house, but again there are differences within the group. There are undemanding plants which will also tolerate dry air and sun, and those whose life-styles require greater humidity. The majority of all these plants flourish best in light situations out of direct sun, though bromeliads, for instance, vary in their degree of tolerance to the sun. Genera with soft, dark-green foliage need shade in summer; the others, however, are more tolerant of the sun.

Plants for the temperate greenhouse, requiring moderate temperatures, i.e. 50–59°F (10–15°C) in winter and 63–68°F (17–20°C) in summer:

Achimenes, hot-water plant
Ampelopsis, ampelopsis
Ardisia, ardisia
begonia species
Beloperone, shrimp plant
bromeliads*
  *Aechmea**
  Billbergia
  *Cryptanthus**
  *Guzmania**
  *Neoregelia**
  *Nidularium**
  *Tillandsia**
  Vriesea
*Brunfelsia**, brunfelsia
cactus, young plants
Calceolaria hybrids, slipper plant
Camellia, camellia
Cissus antarctica, kangaroo vine
Clerodendrum thomsoniae, glory bower
Crassula falcata, propeller plant
Cyclamen, cyclamen
*Dizygotheca elegantissima**, finger aralia
Fatshedera, ivy tree
ferns*
  *Adiantum**, maidenhair fern
  *Nephrolepis**, sword fern
Ficus elastica, rubber plant
Haemanthus, blood lily
Haworthia, haworthia
Helxine, mind your own business
Hibiscus, hibiscus
Hoya carnosa, wax plant
Hydrangea, hydrangea
Impatiens, busy lizzie
Kalanchoe, flaming katy
Mimosa, sensitive plant
Monstera, Swiss cheese plant
orchid genera, partly*
palms:
  Chamaedorea elegans, parlour palm
  Howea fosteriana, paradise palm
  Phoenix loureiri
Peperomia, peperomia
Pilea species, e.g. *P. microphylla*, artillery plant
Piper, pepper plant
Rhododendron simsii, Indian azalea
Rosa, miniature bush rose
*Sanchezia**, sanchezia
Sansevieria, mother-in-law's-tongue
Saxifraga sarmentosa, mother of thousands
*Scindapsus**, marble queen
*Scirpus**, clubrush
*Selaginella**, creeping moss
Sinningia, gloxinia
Streptocarpus, Cape primrose
Tetrastigma voinierianum, chestnut vine
Tradescantia, inch plant
Veltheimia, veltheimia
Zantedeschia aethiopica, arum lily

* plants which require high humidity

The greenhouse of a real plant enthusiast

Many plants make an impression with their coloured foliage alone.

Warm-house plants, which need 64-68°F (18-20°C) in winter, and flourish most readily at temperatures over 68°F (20°C) in summer:

Anthurium scherzerianum, flamingo flower
Caladium, angels' wings
Cissus discolor, cissus discolor
Codiaeum, croton
Dracaena, dragon tree (coloured species)
ferns:
Asophila australis
Fittonia, fittonia
Gardenia, gardenia
orchid genera
Philodendron
eurobescens, blushing philodendron
hastatum, elephant's ear philodendron
scandens, sweetheart plant

NB all species require high humidity!

Warm area

The plants in the following two groups are the most demanding inhabitants of our greenhouses. They are the warm-house plants, and they need particularly careful attention if they are to thrive and flower. Looking after them demands more precise knowledge about growth and rest phases, watering, ventilation, and humidity requirements.

Plants for a moderately warm house, needing fairly high temperatures, i.e. 59-64°F (15-18°C) in winter and at least 64-68°F (18-20°C) in summer:

Acalypha, red-hot cat's tail
*Aeschynanthus**, lipstick vine
*Aglaonema modestum**, Chinese evergreen
Aphelandra, zebra plant
Asparagus, asparagus fern
Begonia rex, rex begonia
Cissus rhombifolia, grape vine
Clivia, kaffir lily
Cocos weddelliana, coconut palm
*Columnea**, goldfish plant
*Cordyline**, cordyline
*Crossandra**, firecracker flower
*Dieffenbachia**, dumb cane
*Episcia**, lace flower
*Euphorbia pulcherrima**, poinsettia
ferns*:
*Asplenium nidus**, bird's-nest fern
*Blechnum**
*Platycerium**, stag's-horn fern
Hippeastrum, amaryllis
*Ixora**, flame of the woods
*Maranta**, prayer plant
*Medinilla magnifica**, rose grape
*Nepenthes**, pitcher plant
orchid genera, partially*
Saintpaulia, African violet
*Spathiphyllum**, peace lily
*Syngonium**, goosefoot plant

* plants which require high humidity

A hobby room for plant-lovers and collectors of rare species

Orchids

The orchid family includes a large number of genera and species in a wide variety of forms. Many are natives of the tropics and subtropics; others come from temperate zones, from the highlands of tropical mountain areas. Working with these attractive flowering plants is one of the most delightful activities available to a greenhouse gardener. Orchid cultivation is a vast subject. If you want to develop a soundly based understanding of it, you would be well advised to study specialist literature, and to visit specialist nurseries and botanic gardens.

Some orchids are relatively undemanding. Most of this group are hybrids which have been cultivated fairly recently, but it also includes *Phalaenopsis* (moth orchid), *Cymbidium* and *Paphiopedilum* (slipper orchid). It takes rather more care, knowledge and ability to look after the more demanding members of the family. They have differing requirements for position, for moisture, and for heat in winter and in summer. Their rest periods vary, too.

A display of tropical splendour: orchids are a favourite in the specialist's greenhouse.

Supplying their nutrient needs is a little science all of its own, because you don't use any of the usual plant fertilisers. Epiphytic orchids, which grow in the branches of trees, have a fundamentally different structure from terrestrial orchids. Even so, an attempt at growing *Cattleya, Dendrobium, Odontoglossum* or *Coelogyne* is thoroughly rewarding.

Bromeliads

The pineapple or bromeliad family, Bromeliaceae, is among the most interesting plant families of the tropical and subtropical areas of South and Central America. Most of them grow as epiphytes in the tops and branch-forks of primeval forest trees, without penetrating the wood with their roots. They often grow alongside orchids, ferns, and Araceae (e.g. anthuriums). You can make a 'bromeliad tree' in the greenhouse to provide a home for such epiphytes as *Guzmania*, *Aechmea*, *Vriesea* and *Nidularium* — but take care not to overload it with plants. If the branches you're using aren't ideally shaped for the task in hand, you can modify them by making holes and hollows in them. Wrap the root balls of the epiphyte in moist sphagnum moss and fasten them to the stem; elastic nylon threads can be useful for tying them up.

Looking after the bromeliad tree requires great care. It's important to moisten the plants regularly; greenhouse epiphytes demand high air humidity, just as they would in their natural habitats. A misting system is the best method for this.

Bromeliads are among the most interesting plants from the tropical and subtropical regions.

Cacti

For lovers of these plants, the range can't be big enough. The family is divided into about 150 genera and over 2,000 species. With all this diversity, their treatment and care call for an equally diverse range of different procedures. If you're a beginner, the notes that follow can't do more than set up a few signposts.

Cacti can tolerate full sunlight but prefer a little shade, especially when they're young. In general, plants that are thickly covered with hair or spines tolerate the sun better than cacti with leaves (and any member of the family that has unprotected green flesh).

Water cacti with caution during their rest period. Often a few drops will be enough, and they shouldn't be allowed to fall on the plant itself. In summer cacti need plenty of water, but they'll be happy with a quarter of the amount of water that other plants demand. Spray them occasionally in spring and summer, but keep them drier from August onwards, to prepare them for winter. Their rest period lasts from late autumn to spring. The exception, however, proves the rule: winter-flowering cacti such as *Zygocactus* (Christmas cactus) or *Rhipsalis cereuscula* (coral cactus) don't require a rest in winter — they take it after they've flowered.

Cacti and succulents need light during their resting phase too, when a temperature of 46-54°F (8-12°C) will be

Cacti flourish in the cool and temperate areas of the greenhouse.

adequate. However, don't let it fall below 43°F (6°C).

A special fertiliser is available to take care of the cacti's nutrient requirements: it contains less nitrogen and more phosphoric acid and potash than other flower fertilisers. Cacti can be propagated by seed, cuttings and grafting.

For seed propagation you'll need an air temperature of 59-68°F (15-20°C) and base heat of 68-77°F (20-25°C) and up to 86°F (30°C). Make sure the humidity is high enough. Sow the seed in spring, in sandy leaf mould arranged in flat pans. Cacti need light to germinate, so use a layer of fine sand that barely covers the seeds — you should still just be able to see them. Prick them out, treat them with scrupulous care, protect them from direct sunlight and from pests and diseases, and water them correctly — all these things will assist the development of the seedlings. In winter too the young plants need more warmth, with temperatures of 54-59°F (12-15°C).

If you're using cuttings for propagation, be sure to let the cut surface of the cutting or offset dry out and callous slightly before inserting it in very sandy rooting compost. Rooting can take up to three weeks in summer and correspondingly longer in winter. Base heat helps to speed up root formation.

Some types of cactus have to be propagated by grafting; with others grafting is used because they grow too slowly on their own roots. However, not every root stock goes with every scion; consult the specialist literature for detailed guidance.

Succulents

By and large, these are treated in much the same way as cacti. In the summer many succulents prefer a place in the open air, and can be put in containers in the garden or on the patio.

The best-known succulents include *Agave, Aloe, Ceropegia, Crassula, Echeveria, Euphorbia* (milkweed), *Gasteria, Haworthia, Mesembryanthemum, Rochea, Stapelia* (carrion flower) etc. In winter most of them prefer a well-lit positions with only moderate warmth, with temperatures of 46-50°F (8-10°C).

You could enrich your display of rare plant specimens by turning it into an aviary. It's also possible to incorporate moving water in the form of a fountain, perhaps with additional lighting. You could even install an aquarium or a fish pond.

A place for your houseplants

Houseplants have to spend their lives in the usually dry atmosphere of a centrally heated room. If you have a greenhouse you can take the opportunity to give them a restorative holiday in more congenial conditions. If your greenhouse is tall enough, houseplants that have outgrown the living room can take up permanent residence there. If the greenhouse ridge isn't much higher than the ceiling indoors, then the really tall plants can be shortened a little.

Air layering is a popular way of rejuvenating plants such as the rubber plant: it's used to persuade the top of the plant to form roots before it is cut off. Just under a leaf, make a slanting cut halfway into the stem. Pack moist sphagnum moss in and around the wound, and cover the whole area with clear plastic. After some weeks, the top of the plant will have formed so many roots that it can be cut from the parent plant and potted up.

A greenhouse offers ideal conditions for most houseplants if you're prepared to spend a little more on heating. The lighting and humidity are better for them than those in the house, and it's easier to keep an even temperature. Ideally a houseplant should stay in the greenhouse after repotting, until it's got used to the bigger pot. That way the plant will acclimatise to the house more easily, and cope with its window-sill existence more readily.

If your greenhouse is equipped with a propagation bed (preferably with base heat), it's possible to take cuttings from the houseplants, too, and to root them successfully. The majority of them root at 57–68°F (14–20°C), but rubber plants need around 79°F (26°C). It's also a good idea to divide plants in the greenhouse; and to let them stay there for a while afterwards to re-establish themselves. In this way you can increase your stock of plants, producing spare plants for exchange or to give away.

To be surrounded by plants is the ambition of every greenhouse gardener.

Winter quarters

A greenhouse is the ideal place to overwinter various plants that would otherwise be very difficult to get through the cold season. Container-grown plants that have already achieved a substantial size would normally present the greatest problems.

Most container-grown plants (e.g. standard marguerites and fuchsias) should be cut back by about one-third before you move them into the greenhouse. Oleander is overwintered with its buds well-formed.

Transfer the plants to your cool or temperate greenhouse as late in the season as possible, but don't allow the frost to get to them. In any case their ability to withstand the cold varies very widely.

There are a few basic rules for overwintering plants. Before you move them in, check them for possible pest infestation and treat them as required. Their new position should be light and cool, but frost-free. Water them very sparingly, especially in the frost-free area. Whatever you do, avoid waterlogging them, which can cause root damage by rotting. Humidity and temperature need to be appropriate. Don't allow the plants to dry out completely, and don't encourage them to make new growth by keeping things too cool. Don't forget to ventilate the greenhouse on sunny days: the temperature can rise very suddenly. And give them 'cool conditions' at other times as well — automatic vent openers are very useful for this. Give the plants more water just before they're due to move outside again in the spring.

Check all overwintering plants regularly, including balcony plants such as geraniums and fuchsias etc. Remove any wilted or diseased foliage, clean them, and cut off any parts that are dry.

Bulbs and tubers should also be overwintered in the frost-free area of the greenhouse. The riper they are, and the drier your storage conditions, the fewer you will lose. It's mostly dahlias, tuberous begonias, cannas and gladioli which are stored in boxes under the staging ready for the next season. Don't forget to label them so you'll know the variety and colour.

Biennial vegetables can also be overwintered in the cool house. Chinese cabbage, cauliflower and endive can be lifted from the outdoor beds complete with their root balls and planted temporarily in the greenhouse. So can leeks, although the check to their growth may cause seed hoods to form.

Accepted average overwintering temperatures are:
37°F (3°C) for yuccas;
41°F (5°C) for citrus plants, pomegranates, agaves and *Plumbago* (leadwort);
43-46°F (6-8°C) for *Agapanthus* (African lily), oleander, bay, myrtle, eucalyptus, *Phoenix* (date palm), *Datura* (angels' trumpets), geraniums;
up to 50°F (10°C) for *Chrysanthemum frutescens* (marguerite) etc.;
Abutilon, heliotrope, *Lantana*, verbenas and fuchsias.

Container-grown plants in their winter home.

Force now, harvest early

Some plant genera can be forced. This means that by taking the right measures you can bring forward their cropping or flowering period.

Vegetables, herbs and fruit

You can have fresh **chives** virtually all winter. Lift clumps in the autumn, let the frost work on them and take them into the greenhouse in succession. Treating them with warm water at about 105°F (40°C) will encourage new growth. Plant the clumps of chives in pots; they can also be dug in under the benching to make full use of the available space.

Parsley roots can be treated in much the same way. Pot them up and put them in the greenhouse, either on the benching or under it. They can also be planted in the ground underneath, again making full use of space. If the roots are stored in a cool place, they can be forced in succession.

The same applies to **onion greens**, and **rhubarb** too is handled in a similar way. It's a good idea to dig up a supply of crowns in the autumn to meet predicted requirements. You can then bring them into the greenhouse just a few at a time, and the warmth there will 'force' them into growth.

If **dandelion roots** are dug up in November they can also be planted in the greenhouse. Put them under the benching, but first cut the leaves back to a height of 1 in (2 cm). You can achieve a successional crop by bringing in the roots in containers, e.g. 2-2.5-gallon (10-12-litre) buckets. Simply prepare several buckets with roots in late autumn, store them in a cool place and set them in the greenhouse as required. Note that the containers must have drainage holes. The layer of earth in the container should be just over 1 inch (3 cm) deep so that root hairs can form. Put in the roots, close together, fill the spaces between them with earth, water them very thoroughly and put the earth on top. Secure a black plastic sheet over the bucket to exclude light and promote blanching. Alternatively you can upend another container on top of it: that way there's no need for a deeper covering layer of earth. As with all the plants mentioned so far, the warmer the temperature, the sooner the crop will be ready — in this case in four weeks at 59°F (15°C).

If you like to experiment, have a go with potatoes: sprout them in mid-January, plant them in mid-February, and finally lift them at the beginning of May.

Chicory is treated in much the same way. Bring in the roots in containers, or plant them in the greenhouse border or under the benching. Chicory is sown in the middle of May and harvested from October; the chicons will be ready to cut 4-5 weeks after you start to force them.

You can also produce an early crop of **potatoes**, but it's best to try it quite early in the year. From January onwards, put a 1-2 in (3-5 cm) diameter tuber into a bucket, and cover it with earth to a depth of 4 in (10 cm). If you have several tubers, bring each of them up to a temperature of 64°F (18°C) in succession, as needed. The warmer it is, the sooner the crop will be ready; three tubers should yield around 6.5 lb (3 kg).

Strawberries can also be forced. It's done by putting plants in 3.5-in (9-cm) pots in the summer, and transferring them to 5-in (13-cm) pots later on, plunging the pots in the garden and keeping them watered and fed. Reduce their water and stop feeding them from October onwards. In December, bring them into the greenhouse at 50°F (10°C), and increase the temperature. Soil or localised heating is an advantage here. The flowers must be hand-pollinated, either with a brush or by shaking the flower stalk or plant, as you would with tomatoes. Until the fruit sets, feed the plants with organic or mineral liquid fertiliser and water them generously, but use a trickle system so that leaves and flowers can stay dry and avoid the danger of rot. The fruit ripens between April and May, depending on the temperature and variety.

Something different for once — greenhouse strawberries grown in pots, and ready to pick in April.

Forcing flowering bulbs

If you're prepared to spend some money on heating, you can enjoy an early spring harvest that has nothing to do with the dictates of the calendar. If you want pots and bowls full of flowering bulbs as early as the end of December or beginning of January, you'll need to start your preparations in September. It's best to buy prepared bulbs from the garden centre or nursery; these have been subjected to a special temperature treatment. In October look out the bowls and pots, cover the drainage holes with a thin layer of gravel or small potsherds to ensure free drainage, and fill them with compost or bulb fibre (peat, shell and charcoal).

Press the bulbs gently into the compost; ideally they should be spaced so they don't touch each other or the pot. Plant them fairly shallowly, so the tips of the bulbs are level with the rim of the container; plant crocuses rather deeper. Finally fill up with compost or fibre, firm and water.

For the next two to three months cover the bulbs with a

deep layer of peat or straw and keep them as cool as possible in a shed, a basement, or at the base of a north-facing wall. A greenhouse (even an unheated one) is not a suitable place for rooting: the temperature varies too much. Coolness is vital during the early stages. It encourages root growth before the bulbs are forced into flowering.

The bulbs root best in the dark, at a temperature of 41–46°F (5–8°C). Bring them into the greenhouse when the shoots are about 2 in (5 cm) long, and raise the temperature to 64–68°F (18–20°C). It will be another two to three weeks before they flower.

It's worth trying to get **lilies-of-the-valley** to flower earlier. These are grown from 'pips', which can be bought in garden centres and nurseries. Simply shorten the roots, and then plant the pips in 6-in (15-cm) deep pots, cover them with moss, and keep them at 68°F (20°C). They should be sprayed with water every day. After the leaves have developed, or when the buds are just emerging from the enclosing leaves, remove the moss. When flowering starts, reduce the temperature to 54–59°F (12–15°C). At these temperatures the flowers last particularly well, about four weeks. You can also buy pips that have been 'pre-treated' (i.e. kept below freezing for 10–12 weeks); these can be brought into growth very quickly without any further pre-treatment other than balling up.

A very early dahlia, courtesy of the greenhouse

Planting **canna** rhizomes in medium-sized pots in February is a well-tried procedure. In April, transfer them to 6-in (15-cm) diameter containers, and water and feed them generously as they continue to grow.

Dahlias naturally come into flower later in the year, but you can bring flowering forward to June. Divide the rhizomes and set them in containers in March. Keep them moist, and grow them on and plant them out in the middle of May, when they are well developed. Alternatively you can plant them in a greenhouse border so that they flower very early.

From the middle of February until March, **tuberous begonias** should be put in compost-filled pans with the smooth, round side downward (and the little hollow on top), then covered with about 1 in (2–3 cm) of growing medium. Keep them moist, and when the first shoots show, put them in a lighter position. Use a knife to divide large tubers into two to four sections. Treat the cut surface with charcoal or with fungicide. Once the roots and leaves have formed, transfer the plants to 4-in (10-cm) pots and plant them out after the middle of May, when all risk of frost has passed. Alternatively, pot them on to flower in the greenhouse.

Flowering branches can also be brought forward in the warm greenhouse, by putting them in a bucket in a light place. This can't usually be done much before December, because they must have a period of cold before they're ready to bloom again. The only suitable branches are those of trees and bushes which bloom naturally in the spring. The easiest way to recognise the flower buds on the branches is by the fact that they're rather fatter and not as pointed as the leaf buds.

Garden frames

A garden frame will help you to raise young plants in the spring, and after that there are plenty of uses for it right through to the winter. It also provides a home for biennial vegetables. A 5-ft (1.5-m) wide frame is easy to manage. If your garden frame is on a permanent site it can be built of wood or concrete; deciding where to put it is normally a quicker process than choosing the site for a greenhouse. To make the best use of the available light, a simple garden frame should be placed in an east-west alignment with the slope of the lights to the south.

The traditional (permanent) 'raised hot bed' of the old type has a hole up to 20 in (50 cm) deep. This is filled with packing material (usually rotting horse manure) that produces heat. Don't set out any plants until the fermentation cools off a little — they could be damaged.

A four-light garden frame with each light 3 × 5 ft (1 × 1.5 m), giving an area of 60 sq ft (6 m^2), is adequate for a family of four. DIY gardeners are happy to put together portable garden frames for themselves, and there are some prefabricated frame designs that are easy to assemble. There are also various possible ways to make portable garden frames using cement 'sockets' and boards which slide into them. Totally transparent designs covered with glass or plastic admit plenty of light, but in summer the sunlight is often too strong. As they are portable, they can be moved to a shady site.

Compared with wooden frames, galvanised metal frames need less maintenance. They come in a different size — 2 ft 8 in × 5 ft (80 × 150 cm) — and they can have non-electric automatic vents, so they don't need constant attention. Self-ventilating garden frame lights mean that you're not always reaching for the wooden wedges, so they're indispensable for anyone who works during the day. Since they don't need electricity or any other form of power, you can also install them as an afterthought; using them means that you can avoid plant damage from temperatures that are too high or too low.

To heat the frame, it's possible to connect it to the domestic heating system, or to use electric heating cables. Think about the connections you're likely to need when choosing the site for your garden frame.

The more intensively a garden frame is used, the greater its value to the gardener.

It's unlikely that anyone would set out with the idea of growing a single type of plant (e.g. vegetables) in a frame. In my experience many people like to use them for raising seedlings, and in autumn you can grow all kinds of root vegetables in the frame: carrots, celery, scorzonera, and leeks and cabbage too, if there's enough room.

Unheated garden frame (cold frame)

With no source of warmth, this frame can only be used to raise plants once the sun is shining in strongly enough to provide nat-

ural heating. The date when you can start using a cold frame will vary from one area to another.

Ventilation is very important by day (I recommend automatic vent openers); at night cover the frame with special mats, which conserve the heat gained from the sun during the day for as long as possible. Supplementary insulation measures (e.g. sheets of expanded polystyrene or even old carpets) will at least make it a little harder for the cold to get in.

Semi-warm garden frame

Depending on the amount of warmth available from your heat source (whether technological or biological) cultivation starts earlier here. With biological methods, a heat-producing base layer of rapidly fermenting organic matter (e.g. fresh horse manure) is packed into the frame; however, unlike heating produced by electricity, or by your domestic hot water system, this warmth is not even and continuous. This isn't much of a problem, since the natural warmth increases as the year wears on. However, because there's a risk that fermenting organic matter may damage the plants, mains-voltage heating cables have almost entirely replaced biological methods.

The construction of the semi-warm frame must be stable. The temperature will be in the region of 50-63°F (10-17°C). As with the unheated frame, it's important to ventilate, and to prevent loss of heat at night. The same goes for the warm frame.

Above *Wooden garden frame with lights raised for taller plants*
Left *Aluminium garden frame with all-round glazing*

Warm garden frame

This frame must be of stable construction, with a hole inside that's large enough to hold packing material to a depth of 20 in (50 cm). As it is normally brought into use in February, it must be possible to keep the temperature at a steady 63-72°F (17-22°C) by means of soil and cable warming until natural sunlight shining in can produce the necessary heat.

Gardeners who'd like to plant lettuce or kohl rabi in late January or early February must be able to provide light, air, moisture and heat in a carefully judged balance. Thermostatically controlled artificial heating offers good controllability and a constant temperature. Insulating materials are necessary here too.

Plastic film

A covering known as a **floating mulch** protects seed and plant beds and speeds up germination and growth. If it's laid on the beds straight after sowing and/ or planting, it results in an earlier harvest; depending on the region, you can gain as much as three weeks. Apart from that, the plants are protected from temperatures below freezing. Another advantage of a floating mulch is that it prevents birds from eating the crop; in the case of fleece, cabbage- and carrot-fly attacks are also reduced, if not entirely stopped, because the flies can't get through the fleece to deposit their eggs. Covering perennial crops such as rhubarb and asparagus can advance the harvest by up to a fortnight. If you combine fleece and perforated film (laid on top of the fleece for two or three weeks) to give a double layer, you can have the harvest even earlier.

Plastic film

Film perforated with holes (0.05-mm gauge polythene): the best standard perforation has proved to be 500 1-cm diameter holes per m2. Effectively this means that 4 per cent of the total area is providing ventilation. The greater the number of holes per m^2, the less the harvest is advanced, but the longer the film can stay in position. The fewer the holes per m^2, the shorter the time the plants can stay covered. Water from rain (or from watering) can always get in through the holes.

Film perforated with slits: also known as 'growing film', this has 30,000 tiny slits per m^2, which mean that it's elastic and can easily be stretched. When the film is laid on the beds the slits are closed, but as the plants grow the film stretches. As a result ventilation is increased by as much as 25 per cent in the final stage. This increase in ventilation matches the growth of the plants, so the temperature under the film gradually comes to match that outside. Even when the slits are closed, water from rain and watering gets in through the film; as the slits open up, the permeability increases.

Ripening hoods: Various polythene protection devices, already popular on the continent, are gradually coming onto the market in this country. These hoods, intended for tomatoes, aubergines and sweet peppers, are made of plastic film perforated with holes or slits to match the requirements of the plants. The same applies to air-permeable fleeces. Don't use a closed film cover under any circumstances, because of the increased humidity and the risk of fungal diseases. The plants must not be kept covered for the whole of their growing season.

Tunnel cloches: these are made from wire hoops covered

These garden frame lights open and shut automatically, without electricity.

with perforated plastic film, and have a wide variety of uses. In this respect they play a role similar to garden frames, and need the same sort of attention as regards ventilation and watering.

Cloches: Cloches made from glass sheets held together with clips were very popular at one time, but it was always all too easy to break the glass. Today they have been largely replaced by a wide range of plastic cloches. Unfortunately some of them are so lightweight that they must be very well secured to stop them blowing away.

Film-covered frames: you can build these yourself. They can be used for various purposes, e.g. housing taller plants. Dahlias and other frost-tender plants can be saved from the first frost in autumn by building a covered frame over them. I recommend using 720-gauge film; 0.8 × 1.2 in (2 × 3 cm) wooden battens are adequate to make the frame. Don't fasten the film directly onto the battens, or it will tear on the edges. Instead fold the edges of the film by turning them over on themselves, then attach them to the battens using roofing-felt nails or non-rusting staples; there must be a layer of plastic or cardboard strip or rubber sheet between the nail-head or staple and the film. For preference (and greater security) cover the frame with additional battens, so the film is embedded between the frame and the securing batten all the way around.

Left *A floating mulch of perforated plastic film*

Right *Ripening hoods for tomatoes should be perforated with holes or slits, or alternatively they could be of air-permeable fleece.*

Shading plastics: A wide range of shading plastics is available for commercial greenhouse gardeners, and is gradually entering the amateur market, too. Some of them are aluminised to reflect light, and so reduce the amount of heat that reaches the plants. Other types of reflective plastic are also being tested. The main drawback is the high cost of these materials.

Fleece

This is permeable across its entire surface; light, air and water from rain and watering can all penetrate it. Its permeability to air is similar to that of perforated film, and it admits around 75 per cent of light as against the 90 per cent with plastic film. This is because the interlinked, fabric-like material is less transparent than film. The air and soil underneath it are not heated as much as they would be under perforated film. When the temperature drops markedly, dew (and moisture rising in the soil) form a thin layer of ice, reducing the loss of warmth from the soil. This protective ice shell protects plants under fleece down to temperatures of 19–23°F (-7 to -5°C). Plants will get off to a better start with film, but fleece can be left in position longer. The light, permeable fleece doesn't blow about as much in the wind, and doesn't do any damage by flapping against the plants.

All these materials should be laid lightly over the growing area — without any kind of tension — and with sensible consideration for the future growth of the plants. Fasten down the edges, ideally with special pegs. Alternatively (in the case of film) you can use a continuous layer of earth or stones or (in the case of fleece) earth or stones at intervals. Make sure beforehand that you have provided any necessary nutrients. As for picking the right time to remove the floating mulch, there's no substitute for your own experience. Slit-perforated film and fleece can both be left on the plants right up to harvesting.

A fleece-covered tunnel cloche.

Protective nets keep off voracious pests such as cabbage flies, flea beetles and cabbage whites.

Nets

Protective nets are an effective way of helping to guard against animal pests in the vegetable garden. Their great advantage is that they're environmentally friendly. You can cover plants such as oriental radish, kohl rabi and carrots with nets. Nets must be laid immediately after sowing or planting, and the perimeter must be absolutely secure, so there is nowhere for animals to creep through. Secure the net with earth or stones all the way around.

Synthetic nets are usually made from polyethylene (polythene). Like fleece or plastic film, they are laid over the beds as a flat covering. The synthetic threads are stable in ultra-violet light, and are woven together in a lattice structure, with a warp and a weft. Their job is to keep the main species of vegetable fly off your plants; to ensure they stay off, the size of mesh is chosen to stop any eggs being deposited on the crop.

Protective nets from various manufacturers have mesh sizes of 1.35 × 1.35 mm, 1.8 × 1.8 mm and 1.6 × 1.2 mm, and weigh between 56 and 75 g/m². They are supplied in widths of around 2 m (e.g. Netlon). They are said to be tough enough to be used 15-20 times or more.

Nets must match the width of the bed; the most durable nets will stay on the plants throughout the growing season.

Plastic film mulch has many advantages as a soil covering: it improves the condition of the soil, stops it from turning into mud in heavy rain, and raises the soil temperature by 4-9°F (2-5°C).

The results are very beneficial. Harvests are earlier and yields are improved. The layer of air just above the soil is warmer, too: this provides a good microclimate, since it limits the overnight loss of heat by radiation from the soil. Weed growth is also suppressed. Water loss from the soil is reduced because soil remains moist longer when it's covered. The mulch also leads to an improvement in crop quality because fruit lies on the plastic, where it's less likely to rot or get dirty and it's easier to harvest. Apart from cucumbers, melons, tomatoes and sweet peppers, it's mostly strawberries that are planted in film mulches. The best mulches are slit-perforated, because they allow water from watering or rain to penetrate the soil. Use seep hoses for watering under the mulch.

Mulch paper: You can unwind this from the roll and lay it directly on the beds, weighting the edges down. It's increasingly used for annual plants. Mulch paper is manufactured from cellulose, incorporating a small proportion of recycled paper, and is sure to become increasingly important as an environmentally friendly product. The material is permeable to water, rots down and can be dug or rotavated in. It contains no chemical additives.

For planting single plants, there are cabbage discs and mulch mats. These, too, can simply be cut from the roll. Before laying the film, you should manure the soil thoroughly.

Mark the sites for your plants on the sheet with chalk. Using a sharp knife, cut cross-shaped slits on the marks and place the plants in the soil beneath.

Index